# DEAD WHITE WRITER ON THE FLOOR

# DEAD
# WHITE
# WRITER
# ON
# THE
# FLOOR

## DREW
## HAYDEN
## TAYLOR

Talonbooks

Talonbooks
9259 Shaughnessy Street, Vancouver, British Columbia, Canada V6P 6R4
talonbooks.com

Seventh printing: 2021

Typeset in Palatino and printed and bound in Canada
Printed on 100% post-consumer recycled paper

Cover design by Adam Swica

Talonbooks gratefully acknowledges the financial support of the Canada Council for the Arts, the Government of Canada through the Canada Book Fund, and the Province of British Columbia through the British Columbia Arts Council and the Book Publishing Tax Credit.

Library and Archives Canada Cataloguing in Publication
Taylor, Drew Hayden, 1962–
Dead white writer on the floor / Drew Hayden Taylor.

A play.
ISBN 978-0-88922-663-0

I. Title.
PS8589.A885D43 2011          C812'.54          C2010-907125-5

*Dead White Writer on the Floor* premiered at Magnus Theatre, Thunder Bay, Ontario, on January 28, 2010, with the following cast and crew:

BILLY JACK / MIKE
Chris Cound

INJUN JOE / FRED
Gordon Patrick White

KILLS MANY ENEMIES / BILL
Gilbert J. Anderson

OLD LODGE SKINS / JOHN
Ira Johnson

POCAHONTAS / SALLY
Reneltta Arluk

TONTO / JIM
Simon Moccasin

*Director*
Mario Crudo

*Set and lighting designer*
Ted Roberts

*Costume coordinator*
Mervi Agombar

*Stage manager*
Gillian Jones

## Characters

BILLY JACK: Half-breed hero, with a strong sense of justice. Early thirties.

INJUN JOE: Drunk half-breed. He should look beaten down by life.

KILLS MANY ENEMIES: Mighty warrior of the plains.

OLD LODGE SKINS: Wise old Elder.

POCAHONTAS: Beautiful teenage girl.

TONTO: Faithful Indian companion. Mid-thirties.

## Setting

The office or study of a writer, in a house. Lots of books and bookshelves. A window, a desk with a computer, and a closet.

## Time

There's no time like the present.

# Introduction

*Dead White Writer on the Floor* was perhaps the most difficult play for me to write. It certainly took the longest. I must say that it was also one of the most fun projects I have ever had the pleasure to work on. And work on it I did.

It's hard to say when I actually put fingers to keyboard, but I do remember the first workshop taking place during my tenure as artistic director of Native Earth Performing Arts, back in the mid-1990s. After that, it went through a few more workshops (including one at the Bluewater Theatre Festival in Kincardine, Ontario) as I tried to nail down the story, characters, and themes, but it was a tough battle. It seemed the overall picture eluded me. I tend to be what could be called a kitchen-sink dramatist, but I was having trouble finding the kitchen sink in this one.

Especially in the second act. That one was a bugger. I wrestled with it repeatedly. I think I rewrote it completely, turning it inside and out ... maybe five or six times, which is unusual for me. I always prided myself on never starting to write a play until I knew exactly what I wanted to say and how I was going to say it. The first act pretty much stayed consistent, other than the elimination of the opening monologues. Yes, the play originally started with each character coming out and establishing their character with a two- to three-minute monologue, brilliantly and hilariously written. Unfortunately, as it was pointed out to me, with six characters delivering a monologue each, Act One would run twelve to eighteen minutes right off the top. And I repeated it in the second act with the new versions of the characters. During yet another workshop, Richard Rose, Tarragon Theatre's artistic director, pointed out that if I kept all the monologues, the play would be a tad long and a tad static. And most of the information in the monologues could be seeded into the text anyway. So out went my beautiful monologues. A very painful cut, let me assure you. Late at night sometimes, when I'm drunk, I take them out and reread them. And weep.

Why this play took so long to finish, I am not positive. Maybe I wasn't sure exactly what I wanted to say. I mean, I don't usually write postmodern theatre (I am not even sure what it is), let alone one influenced by Pirandello's *Six Characters in Search of an Author*. I just wanted to write something fun and different. And these six characters in the first act are such icons in the world of native literature (as written by white authors), who wouldn't want to put them all together in one room and see what happens? Being a writer, I could do this. But what they ended up morphing into, in the second act, was the problem. At one point I had Tonto running a gay dude ranch (yikes!) and Pocahontas becoming a feminist lawyer specializing in sexual harassment cases (double yikes!) It took a quiet moment of reflection, of trying to find the essences and irony of what this play was about, before I came up with who the characters became. And to quote a book I once read, it was good.

The only major change, other than the metamorphosis of the second act, was the creation of Kills Many Enemies. He was not one of the original characters until, in the mid-2000s, Toronto's Centre for Indigenous Theatre wanted to mount a student production of the play and requested to add more characters, if possible. It was then that the obvious occurred to me. How could I have overlooked such a potentially great character as the bloodthirsty warrior? You may have noticed that he is the only character not given a name from an actual novel or movie. I think I wanted him to represent a range of similar characters, unlike the others, who represent very specific identities. But, if pressed, I guess you could call him Wind in His Hair from the film *Dances with Wolves*.

I also got to play with the way worlds and boundaries crossed over and imprinted themselves on the characters. I would give each character a bit of information or under-standing that he or she would not normally have. I mean … would Injun Joe really know what a "personal pronoun" is? Maybe it was a bit of the dead white writer coming through in his character. Who knows? I don't.

Normally it takes me two weeks to write a first draft, and maybe two or three (occasionally four) more drafts afterwards to make everything work properly. Not this time. This play would not be told before its time. So all in all, this play had a gestation of about thirteen or fourteen years altogether, with one more kick at the can every couple of years, before the illustrious Magnus Theatre saw fit to pluck it from the wastelands of unread, unproduced scripts and give it life. Mario Crudo saw the potential, and the rest, as they say, is history. With the fabulous cast he put together, it was one of the most amazing productions I have ever been a part of. It was one of those rare instances of something being funny but actually having a lot to say and comment on.

Since then as I have tried to have it produced elsewhere, I've noticed a disturbing trend regarding this play. Although Mario loved the play and loved the title, not everyone does. In fact, I've received kind words of concern from people who think the title *Dead White Writer on the Floor* is perhaps a little too aggressive and not very consumer friendly. One artistic director told me she thinks it would alienate her audience and was reluctant to even read it. Years ago when my play *Only Drunks and Children Tell the Truth* toured British Columbia, several performances were cancelled because local people objected to the title. What an odd world. I find titles like this very provocative and interesting. I guess that's why I create them.

Oh well, that's theatre, I suppose. In the end the only thing that matters is the product, which you hold in your hands.

Enjoy the play, and be wary of locked rooms and dead white writers.

DREW HAYDEN TAYLOR
Curve Lake First Nation, 2010

# Act One

*Silence, then the sound of a computer powering up. Then fingers on a computer keyboard. They start slowly, then speed up. Somebody is typing. The lights come up and we are in a large study, the office of a writer, with a large desk centre stage and bookshelves stuffed with books. A man sits at the desk, typing on a computer. His back is to the audience so they are unable to see his face.*

*Lights suddenly flicker, and the stage turns dark. In the dark void, there is a lone anguished cry, then something falling and being dragged. Silence. The lights come up to reveal the entire stage. The lighting and atmosphere are dark and mysterious, ethereal and surreal.*

*Standing around the desk are TONTO, BILLY JACK, KILLS MANY ENEMIES, INJUN JOE, POCAHONTAS, and OLD LODGE SKINS. Surprised to find themselves here, they look around at their strange surroundings.*

TONTO
   This not desert!

KILLS MANY ENEMIES
Where's my horse? My teepee? Who are you?

POCAHONTAS
What a strange place.

INJUN JOE
Oh fuck!

OLD LODGE SKINS
This is a bad omen.

BILLY JACK
I don't know this place. Or any of you.

*A drunk INJUN JOE runs to the door and tries to
open it, but it's locked.*

INJUN JOE
Let me out of here. I gotta get out of here. God help me,
let me out!

POCAHONTAS
I'm scared. Do … do any of you know where John … my
John is?

BILLY JACK
John?!

POCAHONTAS
John Smith. He's sort of my boyfriend. He'd know what
to do.

BILLY JACK
John Smith … that is … that was … you look …
Pocahontas …

POCAHONTAS
Yes, that is what my father calls me. Do I know you?!

BILLY JACK
But that's impossible ...

*INJUN JOE pulls out his knife and tries to pry the door open, with no luck. TONTO sits down comfortably in a chair, waiting. He grabs a magazine and idly thumbs through it.*

INJUN JOE
(*at the door*) You son of a bitch ...

OLD LODGE SKINS
Why are you so angry, my son?

INJUN JOE
I ain't angry and I ain't your son. This ain't right. Not by a long shot.

*He hurts his hand trying to pry open the door.*

INJUN JOE
Goddamn ...!

OLD LODGE SKINS
Relax, my young friend. It is as it should be. As I have seen it.

KILLS MANY ENEMIES
Old man, respected Elder, is this ... this place ... your lodge?

OLD LODGE SKINS
No. I have never been here before.

KILLS MANY ENEMIES
Then why are you so calm?

OLD LODGE SKINS
Being agitated and stabbing a door will not change things. It is obvious where we are.

KILLS MANY ENEMIES
Where are we then, Grandfather?

OLD LODGE SKINS
I am old. It was my time. I have passed on to the next
world. So have all of you, I would guess. I say we rest
and let our spirits become one with the Four Directions.

*He starts to chant.*

INJUN JOE
The hell I have. Look at this. (*shows blood on hand*) You
don't bleed when you're a ghost. At least I don't think
you're supposed to. The last thing I remember is, I was
trapped in a cave but I was still alive.

OLD LODGE SKINS
Hmmm, I see your point. And I must pee. That is not
right either.

*POCAHONTAS takes INJUN JOE's hand and looks
about for something to bandage it with.*

POCAHONTAS
Oh, you have a boo boo.

INJUN JOE
(*interested in the pretty girl*) Yes. Yes, I have a boo boo. A
big boo boo.

KILLS MANY ENEMIES
(*looking at scratch*) That is nothing. The last thing I
remember, I was taking the scalp of a white man with a
long knife. My hands were sticky and wet with his
blood. I had taken many scalps that day. And I have
suffered many wounds over the years. You do not have
a ... big boo boo.

INJUN JOE
Back off, buddy. I say it is.

BILLY JACK
You … you mentioned a cave.

INJUN JOE
And who the fuck are you?

BILLY JACK
The cave … tell me about it.

INJUN JOE
If you gotta know, I was chasing … I mean playing with this brat … I mean young boy in a cave, and somehow, that … the little rascal got away from me.

BILLY JACK
What was his name?

INJUN JOE
His name? I don't rightly know. Sawyer, I think.

BILLY JACK
Tom Sawyer. You're Injun Joe. At least I think you're supposed to be.

INJUN JOE
(*suspicious*) Do you know me, 'cause I sure don't know you.

BILLY JACK
You might not believe …

*KILLS MANY ENEMIES finds the air conditioner in the window. At first he is surprised by the cool air.*

KILLS MANY ENEMIES
Oh that's nice. I like that!

BILLY JACK
  You okay?

KILLS MANY ENEMIES
  Cool air. This may be bad medicine but it sure feels
  good. Very good. It was hot and dusty where I was, and
  buckskin just does not breathe. I want one of these. How
  can I get one?

OLD LODGE SKINS
  Maybe it is a spirit from the north.

TONTO
  That not mustang!

  *Then they all notice TONTO in the corner, drumming
  his fingers, looking bored.*

TONTO
  What? In this book thing, there image of something steel
  and glass. It move very fast, and called Mustang. Look
  like no mustang horse Tonto ever see. Crazy people.

BILLY JACK
  It's called a car.

TONTO
  A car … hey, look, another one. A Cherokee!

KILLS MANY ENEMIES
  You are awfully calm. Too calm. Is all this your magic?
  Are you behind all of this? Must I gut you like a fat
  groundhog?

TONTO
  Me? No? Me just waiting for Kemosabe to save me.

INJUN JOE
  Who the hell is this Kemosabe?

TONTO
Him partner. Whenever Tonto get in trouble, he come
save. Always. (*pause*) Any time now. (*pause*) Any time.

*INJUN JOE spots another door behind TONTO and
goes racing for it.*

INJUN JOE
Another door!? Let me out!

*He pulls it open to reveal a closet, and a dead body
falls out. It is dressed exactly like the writer in the
opening. Only the legs are visible to the audience.*

INJUN JOE
Oh fuck.

KILLS MANY ENEMIES
Hoka!

POCAHONTAS
Is he ... is he?

INJUN JOE
Fuck.

TONTO
Him dead.

POCAHONTAS
How?

*Out of habit, OLD LODGE SKINS lifts his hand in
greeting.*

OLD LODGE SKINS
How.

POCAHONTAS
No. I mean how did that poor man die?

INJUN JOE
Fuck.

BILLY JACK
Will you stop saying that?

INJUN JOE
Don't tell me what to say or do, boy, or you'll be plenty sorry.

TONTO
(*in the corner, getting impatient*) Any time, Kemosabe. Any time.

POCAHONTAS
Does anybody know him?

INJUN JOE
Whoever he was or died from, I didn't do it.

*BILLY JACK kneels and examines the body.*

BILLY JACK
Well, the first thing is, he's a white man.

POCAHONTAS
John?!

TONTO
Kemosabe?!

*Both POCAHONTAS and TONTO go rushing to the body.*

TONTO
Kemosabe and me were just in middle of stopping bank robbery when this … (*examines body too*) Whew, no. Me not screwed.

POCAHONTAS
It's not John either. I was so frightened.

KILLS MANY ENEMIES
A white man's death does not concern me, unless I have slit his throat myself and watched his blood gush out. I turn my back on him.

INJUN JOE
I'm noticing a theme with him.

TONTO
What we do now?

OLD LODGE SKINS
Pray for him on his journey to the spirit world.

*OLD LODGE SKINS starts to chant once more.*

INJUN JOE
Oh shut up. Somebody shut him up.

KILLS MANY ENEMIES
Little man, have you no respect for your Elders? Must I exchange your eyeballs for your testicles?

INJUN JOE
I'm hungover and he's giving me a headache. God, seems like I've had a hangover forever.

KILLS MANY ENEMIES
Yes, you smell of their firewater. You smell of many things. Perhaps you are in league with this man. Perhaps I should fillet you like a trout ...

INJUN JOE
Back off, feather boy.

BILLY JACK
Oh, great warrior, let him live. He is not worth the effort.

KILLS MANY ENEMIES
Very well then. But beware, little man, your scalp may yet hang from my lodgepole.

POCAHONTAS
All this talk of death, I'm frightened.

*The old man bends down with a noticeable grunt, using a staff. He examines the body.*

OLD LODGE SKINS
This man died at the hands of another.

INJUN JOE
Weren't me that did it.

POCAHONTAS
He was killed?! Who … who could have done this horrible thing?

INJUN JOE
Not me.

BILLY JACK
What makes you think he was murdered, Grandfather? Maybe he had a heart attack or a stroke.

OLD LODGE SKINS
I saw it in a vision, as is my way. It was unclear, but I saw him, and he was lying there like this. There is much here I do not understand, but I do know this man is dead because of one of us. The Creator has told me.

KILLS MANY ENEMIES
I care nothing for these white people. But it was not my lance that took his life. Perhaps another warrior did.

TONTO
You think one of us did this?

INJUN JOE
Not me.

BILLY JACK
It seems likely. And the door is locked.

INJUN JOE
I told ya.

TONTO
Me not know anything about where you all come from, but where me lives, one dead white man, six Indians, in locked room—not good beginning.

INJUN JOE
It was one of you! I bet everything I know that one of you people did it!

POCAHONTAS
Not me. I like white men.

TONTO
Me too. Probably different reason though.

INJUN JOE
(*indicating TONTO*) He did it. He's got a gun. He shot him. Dirty, lousy, stinking murderer. Let's hang him!

*BILLY JACK quickly takes TONTO's gun out of its holster and smells the barrel, then checks the six cartridges.*

BILLY JACK

This gun has not been fired recently. And there are no bullet wounds on the body.

INJUN JOE

Maybe he hit the guy with it. Pistol-whipped him. You can do a lot of damage with the barrel of a gun. I know. Or maybe him (*indicating KILLS MANY ENEMIES*) with that pig-sticking spear of his. I know he denies it but …

KILLS MANY ENEMIES

Little man, why do you taunt death so much? The coyotes of the prairies could grow very fat upon your carcass. I have killed many white men. But I have also taken many Indian lives in battle. Mind your tongue or I will cut it out and use it to lace my moccasins.

TONTO

Why you accuse us? You see him, or any here, take man's life?

INJUN JOE

I didn't see nothin'. It wasn't me, so it had to be one of you. That's my reasonin'. I bet it was you! (*indicating BILLY JACK*) Yeah, it was him that did it. Killed this old white fellow. Case closed. Now let's figure a way out of here.

TONTO

Why him?

INJUN JOE

Look at him. He looks white. White people do this to each other all the time.

BILLY JACK

I'm only half-white. Just like you.

INJUN JOE
    But I didn't do it. That's the diff'… how do you know I
    gots white blood?

BILLY JACK
    I read it.

INJUN JOE
    You read it?! Where?

BILLY JACK
    In a book.

INJUN JOE
    I don't know anything about no book. Are you playing
    with me, boy? 'Cause that's a dangerous business. I'd
    hate for you to end up …

OLD LODGE SKINS
    Enough! Harsh words breed harsh actions.

TONTO
    Hmmm, good words.

POCAHONTAS
    (*to BILLY JACK*) Did you kill him?

BILLY JACK
    No.

KILLS MANY ENEMIES
    Your skin might be white, but your heart is indeed red. I
    will spare you your life. (*to INJUN JOE*) You … I have
    not decided yet.

INJUN JOE
    I ain't afraid of you.

KILLS MANY ENEMIES
    Then you are foolish, as well as ugly.

POCAHONTAS
(*to BILLY JACK*) Oh good. I'm so glad you didn't kill him. I didn't want to be afraid of you. (*looks at the body*) He's kind of a nice-looking man, don't you think? As white men go.

TONTO
Yes. Plenty strong features. Good chin. Nice dimples.

POCAHONTAS
My father wanted to kill a white man once, but I wouldn't let him.

BILLY JACK
John Smith.

POCAHONTAS
That was him. Such a strong and memorable name, don't you think? John Smith.

TONTO
Hmm, my friend Kemosabe never kills anybody, white or Indian. Just shoots guns out of their hands.

INJUN JOE
He shoots the guns out of their hands?!

TONTO
Him good shot.

INJUN JOE
What the hell good does shooting the guns out of people's hands do? Him stupid. I've killed a few white people in my day, but only the ones that did me wrong. I got a long memory. (*to BILLY JACK*) How many you put in the ground, boy? I bet your share.

BILLY JACK
My past is my past. Not yours.

OLD LODGE SKINS
   Wise words.

INJUN JOE
   And you, old man. Ever killed a white man?

OLD LODGE SKINS
   Many winters ago, I was once a great warrior … I think.
   My lance was bloody and my heart fearless. But we did
   not meet the white man till many years after I had put
   my war lance down. Though once, when our village
   was attacked by the long knives, I grabbed a gun and
   fired at one riding a horse. But by then, though my heart
   was strong, my eyes were weak and my aim poor. He
   escaped and my village died.

POCAHONTAS
   You remind me of my father. Brave and wise.

OLD LODGE SKINS
   My heart thanks you, little one.

   *KILLS MANY ENEMIES goes into his monologue
   state.*

KILLS MANY ENEMIES
   Enough! I grow weary of this talk. My heart is young
   and my anger hungry. If we must battle our way out of
   here, then let it begin. I am not afraid to face whoever
   hides from us or whoever killed this white man. Let
   them die under my tomahawk. Let my lodgepole be
   covered with their scalps. Let the wind carry my battle
   songs to the Four Directions, for I am not afraid. My
   name is Kills Many Enemies and my name rings true!

   *There is silence.*

TONTO
   Who him talking to?

INJUN JOE
   No idea.

POCAHONTAS
   (*indicating the body*) Should we just leave him lying there like that? He looks so sad and lonely.

KILLS MANY ENEMIES
   Let him rot in the sun. Let the maggots enjoy his pasty flesh. Let the birds pick his bones clean.

POCAHONTAS
   Eww.

KILLS MANY ENEMIES
   Let the winds blow the dust from his bones far from our sacred lands. Let …

BILLY JACK
   I think we need a more immediate plan.

TONTO
   So what we do now, Kemo … sorry. Habit. Ah, what we do now, then?

BILLY JACK
   You can do things without him, you know.

TONTO
   It just come so naturally. Hard to stop. So what we do, then?

BILLY JACK
   What do you think we should do?

TONTO

Me? Me never have to come up with plan. You think one up, you part white. White people good for that kind of thing.

BILLY JACK

No. You try.

TONTO

Uh, you hungry? Me can maybe cook something. Who up for some gopher?

INJUN JOE

Me.

BILLY JACK

No. You must adjust. You are in a different time and place. You are here now. You are equal to each of us. You don't have to follow him anymore.

TONTO

Me don't understand. You sound like you know Tonto.

INJUN JOE

Yeah, don't he?

BILLY JACK

What I do know is that you can be better than you were. All of you. Maybe all of us. We're obviously here for a reason.

OLD LODGE SKINS

For one so young, you speak much truth. There is a purpose to everything in creation. A purpose why the mighty eagle hunts the prairie dog, a reason why the rains come when they do, a reason for everything. Often times we might not understand that logic, but we may rest assured that there is a design. We six stand here, in this strange place, with a dead white man on the floor. Why?

INJUN JOE

'Cause he (*indicating BILLY JACK*) killed him!

OLD LODGE SKINS

Maybe, maybe not. I do not know what the truth in that matter might be. But one of us killed this poor man. But if we are to solve this great mystery, must we understand why someone would want to take his life? For that, we must learn more about the man. What do we know?

TONTO

Him kind of handsome.

OLD LODGE SKINS

Not what I was expecting, but okay.

INJUN JOE

He gots plenty of books.

BILLY JACK

That's because he's a writer.

POCAHONTAS

A what?

BILLY JACK

A writer. A teller of tales.

INJUN JOE

Hey, how ... how did you know he was a ... what did you say ... a teller of tales? A writer? That's a pretty detailed and specific piece of information to know. You seem to know a lot of things.

BILLY JACK
On his desk, a stack of books with several different titles. But only one name. And the photo on the back … him.

TONTO
Him right.

INJUN JOE
Why would we be locked in a room with a dead white writer? This be gettin' stranger and stranger.

*Everybody looks at each other in confusion.*

KILLS MANY ENEMIES
So what? A dead white man is a dead white man. Who cares what he did in his life? (*to BILLY JACK*) My brother, if you do not want his scalp, then I will take it. For my knife is sharp and well practised.

*He kneels down, pulling out his knife, but POCAHONTAS grabs his arm.*

POCAHONTAS
Noble warrior, please don't.

KILLS MANY ENEMIES
Why not? What is this man to you?

POCAHONTAS
Nothing, but that would be icky.

KILLS MANY ENEMIES
What is "icky"? I do not know this word "icky."

POCAHONTAS
It means … I mean … it's … not a very nice thing to do. And I'm all about being nice.

INJUN JOE

I bet you are. What do you think has happened here, sweet cheeks?

POCAHONTAS

Well, maybe … maybe this man died because of love. The only marks left by love are on the heart. Back in the forest, I once saved a life for love. I don't know much about these things, but wouldn't it be just as easy to take a life for love?

BILLY JACK

Some might say love has taken more lives than it has created.

TONTO

Hmm, wise words wisely spoken.

INJUN JOE

Will you shut up with that? It's getting on my nerves.

TONTO

Me sorry.

BILLY JACK

One small problem. Who did this man love, or who loved this man, that would cost him his life, and more importantly, would get us involved?

INJUN JOE

What would you know about love?

BILLY JACK

Enough.

POCAHONTAS

I know about love.

INJUN JOE
    I bet you do.

POCAHONTAS
    Love makes the sun rise, the rivers flow, the birds sing.
    It makes the heart sing. Love is everything.

TONTO
    For you, maybe.

POCAHONTAS
    You don't agree?

TONTO
    No want talk about it. Hurt too much.

POCAHONTAS
    Oh, you sound bitter. That's so sad. Can I help?

TONTO
    We swim different rivers. Let me leave at that.

KILLS MANY ENEMIES
    (*to BILLY JACK*) Why does he talk like that? It is
    confusing.

POCAHONTAS
    How tragic. Maybe this man died because he had no
    love in his life. I know I would die.

INJUN JOE
    I got some love for you.

BILLY JACK
    No you don't.

INJUN JOE
    Just trying to be friendly.

POCAHONTAS
Its okay. I'll be your friend. I'm everybody's friend.
Have you ever heard the wind call your name?

INJUN JOE
Not sober.

BILLY JACK
Your kindness is wasted there.

POCAHONTAS
Kindness is never wasted.

BILLY JACK
Neither is vigilance.

KILLS MANY ENEMIES
(*frustrated*) Yes, yes, the girl is very pretty. (*indicating
INJUN JOE*) He is not to be trusted. (*to BILLY JACK*)
You are her protector. That is all rather obvious, but that
is not important to me. I want to get out of here. I want
to feel the prairie wind again. There are soldiers waiting
to be ambushed. Settlers to be massacred. This place is a
box and Kills Many Enemies does not belong in a box.
Can we move on and find different hunting grounds?!

POCAHONTAS
How? He said the door is locked. I don't know what we
should do!

OLD LODGE SKINS
Come, little one. Sit by me. You can help keep an old
man warm while we decide.

INJUN JOE
Sure. He gets to sit with her. Why don't you all mind
your own business? She's a grown woman.

*BILLY JACK picks up a pencil. He places it right in front of INJUN JOE's face and breaks it in half.*

BILLY JACK

The sound of your bones breaking.

INJUN JOE

Leave me alone.

TONTO

Hmm, him trouble.

OLD LODGE SKINS

Not all arrows fly true.

INJUN JOE

Oh give it a break! "Him trouble." You mak'em good point. Jesus, try using a personal pronoun properly for once. You might like it. And what's with the "not all arrows fly true"? What the hell is that supposed to mean? "Not all arrows fly true." Talk to me like a real person. Enough with the "my heart soars like an eagle" mumbo jumbo. Try to be like a real and true person.

BILLY JACK

A real and true person …

KILLS MANY ENEMIES

What is "mumbo jumbo"?

OLD LODGE SKINS

You have a lot of anger in you, my son. Perhaps you are the man who took the writer's life. You have a desperate look about you.

POCAHONTAS

Did you kill the white writer?

INJUN JOE

No. I ain't got no love for white people or most Indian people, but that ain't my work. I use this.

*He holds up a knife then puts it away.*

INJUN JOE

And there ain't no knife marks on him. Go ahead and look.

*POCAHONTAS kisses him on the cheek.*

POCAHONTAS

Good. I'm glad you didn't kill him either. I think you try to be a lot meaner than you actually are. I believe in the inherent goodness of everybody. It is my way.

*POCAHONTAS wanders away. INJUN JOE watches her longingly. TONTO is nearby.*

INJUN JOE

Look at those fringes shake.

*TONTO gives her a glance but doesn't really react.*

INJUN JOE

What's with you anyways? That's one fine woman walkin' away. Your headband a little too tight?

TONTO

Pretty woman all right.

INJUN JOE

That's all you can say! Women like her were created to be looked at. I've even caught the do-gooder over there giving her the occasional glance. If the old man didn't have cobwebs under his loincloth, he'd be shaking his lance at her. But not you. Why not?

TONTO
    I said pretty woman.

INJUN JOE
    I don't get you. I mean, you'd think after all those nights
    in the desert with the masked man, just the two of you,
    alone, week after week, month after month, doing his
    laundry, cooking for him, always together …

    *He pauses. The proverbial light bulb goes off over
    INJUN JOE's head as the obvious occurs to him.*

INJUN JOE
    Ahhh …

TONTO
    What?

INJUN JOE
    I got it. It's so obvious. Never mind. Moving on.

TONTO
    What?

INJUN JOE
    Let's just say, you two ride double, and leave it at that.

    *INJUN JOE walks away. All the while, BILLY JACK
    is closely examining the books on the shelves.*

TONTO
    What?

    *POCAHONTAS joins KILLS MANY ENEMIES,
    who is staring at the computer on the desk.*

POCAHONTAS
    What are you looking at?

KILLS MANY ENEMIES
 I do not know. Like many things in this strange place, I
 do not know its nature. What do you think it is? Should
 I kill it?

POCAHONTAS
 It makes a noise, like bees, only softer.

OLD LODGE SKINS
 Beware its sting.

KILLS MANY ENEMIES
 Whatever it is, do not fear it. I will protect you. All of
 you. For I am Kills Many Enemies.

OLD LODGE SKINS
 Yes. We know. You've told us. Many times.

POCAHONTAS
 What is that, across its front?

OLD LODGE SKINS
 It is the white man's writing. I saw such scratchings
 once when Black Robes gave me a book about a
 medicine man named Jesus. They are only markings. A
 way of telling stories. Talking. Like smoke signals, but
 smaller.

INJUN JOE
 You're right. That's writin'. Muscle boy over there said
 the dead guy had something to do with writin' and
 books. This might be the answer.

POCAHONTAS
 The answer to what?

INJUN JOE
 To everything. (to BILLY JACK) You can read this, can't
 you?

BILLY JACK
 Yes.

INJUN JOE
 What does it say?

> *BILLY JACK, his arms full of books, approaches them.*
> *He puts the books down and examines the computer*
> *screen.*

BILLY JACK
 It is some sort of story. About Indians.

POCAHONTAS
 I love stories. Is it a love story?

BILLY JACK
 I'm not sure. I can only read what's on this screen.

KILLS MANY ENEMIES
 Want me to stab it? It might have spurting blood.

TONTO
 What happen in story?

BILLY JACK
 I can't tell from this one page, but the title here says *The*
 *Further Adventures of* ... I think it's about us. It's a
 collection of short stories. According to these notes here,
 there's a dozen or so stories in this thing continuing
 these adventures, featuring each of us.

OLD LODGE SKINS
 I do not understand. What do you mean ... each of us?

BILLY JACK
 It seems you are all characters from books and stories.

INJUN JOE
 And you ain't?

BILLY JACK
    Logic says I am. As are all of you.

    *There is silence.*

KILLS MANY ENEMIES
    No. I am Kills Many Enemies, not some person in a
    story. Touch me. Feel me. I am real. My lance is real. My
    bravery is real. You are wrong.

POCAHONTAS
    The big violent man is right. I am a real person. I'm not
    make-believe …

BILLY JACK
    You were once, but most of that has been lost. You are
    now … as much make-believe as any of us. You are now
    less fact, more … a symbol.

POCAHONTAS
    I am? Nobody told me.

TONTO
    You crazy! Do I look fake?

BILLY JACK
    Let's not go down that road. But everything in this room
    tells me it's true. This thing … (*holds up a DVD case*) … I
    read the back. It's my life story. In ninety minutes. In
    something called Blu-ray.

OLD LODGE SKINS
    If what you say is true, and my heart has not yet told me
    so, why are we here? I know of no legends or teachings
    to explain this to me.

    *BILLY JACK starts going through the books on the
    desk, and tossing them to each of the individual
    characters. They catch them and look through them.*

BILLY JACK
    This is you. This is me. This is all of us.

KILLS MANY ENEMIES
    I do not know these symbols.

INJUN JOE
    I can't read either. You're making this up.

BILLY JACK
    Kills Many Enemies, look at the cover.

    *He does and he sees himself.*

KILLS MANY ENEMIES
    That is me, though I do not think my nose can be that
    big.

TONTO
    Kemosabe and me … it is true.

POCAHONTAS
    He's writing more … You mean, I have to swim in more
    streams? Save more white men? Spend more cold
    winters in this tiny dress?!

BILLY JACK
    It looks that way.

INJUN JOE
    No more, please. It has to end. I can't go back to that
    cave. I'll die, I know it.

POCAHONTAS
    What should we do?

OLD LODGE SKINS
    When travelling in strange lands with strange gods, it is
    best to give such places a wide berth. This machine and
    what this man writes are not our responsibility. We are

all but a web strand in his stories. If we break one, we
might break all. I have spoken.

INJUN JOE
Screw that. You are all forgetting one minor detail.
Those strands you were talking about … they're already
a little shaky. The guy who wove those precious strands
is dead on the floor. Those stories are half-finished. He's
not going to finish them 'cause one of you killed him.
Right or wrong, he's dead. Meaning nobody's going to
finish it. We're stuck here. Any of this sinking in?

POCAHONTAS
Is he right?

> *Everybody looks momentarily confused and worried.*
> *POCAHONTAS goes to the study door. She tries to*
> *open it.*

POCAHONTAS
There must be a way out. I want to go back to my
stream! I was wrong. It's not so bad. I want my animals.
Where is John? He's white. He knows these things. He
should be here to protect us!

OLD LODGE SKINS
Do not fear unnecessarily, little one. This man speaks
only to frighten us like children in a thunderstorm.

TONTO
You think you have all answers. What yours?

INJUN JOE
If what muscle boy over there says is true … finish it
ourselves.

KILLS MANY ENEMIES
Finish what ourselves, little man?

INJUN JOE
The short stories. Write them the way we want. Be who we want.

*There is awed silence.*

POCAHONTAS
Noooo …

OLD LODGE SKINS
That is an evil thought … isn't it?

TONTO
How?

OLD LODGE SKINS
(*holding up hand*) How.

BILLY JACK
But none of us know how to work that thing. We could do more damage than good.

INJUN JOE
Don't care. My whole life has been one of damage. Once you've lived in hell, even purgatory looks good. Take a chance, muscle boy. I say we spit God in the eye.

TONTO
Me no think life can be this easy. Can't be … can it?

INJUN JOE
Why not? This is our chance to do something. Be somebody.

OLD LODGE SKINS
Perhaps, but maybe this was all meant to be. The Creator works in mysterious ways. Death is not so horrible. It is fear of death that terrifies us.

INJUN JOE

But I haven't lived a real life. I've lived a travesty of a real life. I can't be anything other than what is in this book. I reject it. Old man, I don't fear my death, I fear my life. I am going to find an answer. Who's with me?

*Everybody looks awkward, unsure.*

INJUN JOE

Cowards. You're all cowards.

OLD LODGE SKINS

I am not a coward. It is true that the story and the storyteller are one and the same. The storyteller may die, but if the story is strong, it will live forever. And stories can change, and be changed. Like a man.

INJUN JOE

Yeah. Changed.

OLD LODGE SKINS

But you are not a storyteller.

KILLS MANY ENEMIES

And while you and this machine do not frighten me, only a fool battles in the dark. And I am not a fool. I will not help you.

INJUN JOE

Fine, you and the old man suit yourself. I ain't hanging around to be treated like shit.

*Everybody looks uncomfortable. INJUN JOE examines the computer.*

BILLY JACK

What are you doing?

INJUN JOE
Finding a better world. You can all stay here and debate
the mysteries of the universe if you want. Me, I want
something better and I have the means right here to find
it. You can all go to hell, except you (*to POCAHONTAS*)
of course.

POCAHONTAS
Please be careful.

INJUN JOE
You can come with me, you know. Could be fun. Me
and you, against the world. What do you say, sweet
thing?

POCAHONTAS
Sorry, but I don't date Indian men.

INJUN JOE
I'm half white ...

POCAHONTAS
Sorry. Not enough.

INJUN JOE
Then the hell with you too.

OLD LODGE SKINS
Do not dwell on the ...

> *INJUN JOE pushes the old man away harshly.*

INJUN JOE
Keep your wise-Elder stuff to yourself. It don't impress
me. All of you. Be cartoons, be happy running through
the woods like the noble savage. I want more. More than
he would give me. And whichever one of you killed
him, thanks. He deserved it. And I'll be better off for it.

KILLS MANY ENEMIES
This is a waste of time. This man will listen to none of us. I say we destroy this box and be done with it. And then kill him.

*KILLS MANY ENEMIES picks up the computer.*
*INJUN JOE grabs KILLS MANY ENEMIES' knife*
*and threatens him with it.*

INJUN JOE
Listen here, boy. Put that there thing down. Or I'll string you up by your entrails.

KILLS MANY ENEMIES
You would kill me for this humming box?

INJUN JOE
I've killed better men for less. Now put it down nice and slow.

BILLY JACK
Perhaps you'd better put it down.

KILLS MANY ENEMIES
Then may I kill him? You can help. It'll be fun!

*KILLS MANY ENEMIES slowly puts the computer down.*

INJUN JOE
Don't you people see? I'm trying to save your lives or at least change them, as well as mine.

OLD LODGE SKINS
You know nothing of that machine or what it can do. Is your life so horrible that you would risk endangering all of us?

INJUN JOE
Is yours so perfect it couldn't be better?

OLD LODGE SKINS
I am happy with how I will spend my final days. Prairie
as far as my old eyes can see. Enough buffalo robes to
keep my cold body warm. It is truly the way the Creator
meant us to live. It is a good life.

INJUN JOE
Uh-huh. (*to POCAHONTAS*) You. Do you enjoy your
life?

POCAHONTAS
Me? Um … yes … yes, I do. Uh … wouldn't you?

INJUN JOE
I've been playin' poker long enough to know a bluff
when I hear one. (*to TONTO*) And you, I suppose you're
happy riding the range, being the hero's sidekick?

TONTO
Me seen worse ways of living. A lot worse.

INJUN JOE
You one bad liar too. Kills Many Enemies …

KILLS MANY ENEMIES
Yes?

INJUN JOE
I take it where you come from, you're very brave? Well
respected? Lots to eat. Warm place to sleep? Just fight,
be noble, hunt buffalo. Stand tall and regal. Pose for
postcards. You're a happy savage?

KILLS MANY ENEMIES
Yes.

INJUN JOE
 No regrets?

KILLS MANY ENEMIES
 No …

INJUN JOE
 Sure. (*to BILLY JACK*) What about you?

BILLY JACK
 Since the day I was born, there have been precious few
 things that have brought serenity to my heart. Living
 each day is enough. Every night when I close my eyes,
 and I know I have done something to make the
 reservation a safer place, then I allow myself the luxury
 of peace. For me, that is as close to happiness as I can
 get.

INJUN JOE
 Nice speech. Too bad it's a crock of shit.

BILLY JACK
 I'm trying really hard not to get angry at you. But
 sometimes you make it really difficult …

INJUN JOE
 You wanna hit me, muscle boy? Huh, do ya? Then hit
 me if it'll make you feel so …

 *Suddenly, like lightning, BILLY JACK lashes out.*
 *INJUN JOE collapses, struck down. He is both in*
 *pain and surprised. He crawls to his feet.*

INJUN JOE
 He hit me! You hit me!

 *INJUN JOE takes out his knife.*

INJUN JOE
> Stay away from me. All of you. Stay away from me, you
> crazy bastards.

> *BILLY JACK easily disarms him. POCAHONTAS*
> *rushes between them.*

POCAHONTAS
> Both of you, stop it!

BILLY JACK
> This doesn't concern you.

POCAHONTAS
> It concerns all of us. Please don't hurt him. I know he's
> not my brave and handsome John Smith. In fact, he's
> kind of repugnant. But hurting him won't help.

OLD LODGE SKINS
> Listen to the girl. She is small but her words are big.

INJUN JOE
> I ain't afraid of you.

TONTO
> Do not lie. Him big, strong. You weak and repugnant.

INJUN JOE
> I am not repugnant.

TONTO
> Is him repugnant?

> *Everybody nods and answers in agreement.*

KILLS MANY ENEMIES/OLD LODGE SKINS/
POCAHONTAS/BILLY JACK
> Yep. Very. Extremely. Where to begin? Definitely. Don't
> get me started.

INJUN JOE

I see. So I'm repugnant. Let's see you not be repugnant
when you have to make money by digging up graves
for medical schools. Let's see you be sophisticated when
you sleep in barns and caves. Yeah, I'm repugnant while
people think their happy thoughts about you people.
But I'm also the one in this room that wants to get out of
here the most. I'm the one who's had enough. I have
nothing to lose and everything to gain. Being repugnant,
being unwanted, maybe it gives me the strength to walk
away from what I was. It's made me want something
better. I want to be real. Better!

POCAHONTAS

Better ...

TONTO

So much anger.

INJUN JOE

Yes. So much anger. Because you are all liars. All of you.
I may be a worthless old drunk, but at least I'm honest
about it. And I think—no, I know for sure—all of you,
deep down inside, are as pissed off as I am. You're all
just afraid to admit it. I hate this world and what I am in
it. Did you all hear that? I want something more.

TONTO

Like what?

INJUN JOE

I don't know. Maybe go off to one of those fancy schools
they have and learn stuff. Be smarter and more educated
than I am. Than he made me. I deserve better. I deserve
a shot at being as good as any of those white bastards!

POCAHONTAS
I don't like this game. It's scaring me. There must be some other game we can play. I know one where we all try to run through the tree branches like squirrels. It's great fun.

INJUN JOE
Games! You want to play games? Maybe you are who you are supposed to be. Fine. Play your silly games. No more for me. I want out.

*INJUN JOE picks up the keyboard.*

POCAHONTAS
Wait! (*pause*) Is it really possible? I mean about changing.

INJUN JOE
I don't know nothin' for sure, but I aim to find out. Why? You interested?

POCAHONTAS
Maybe.

BILLY JACK
Why?

POCAHONTAS
I have my reasons. Do you think it hurts?

OLD LODGE SKINS
Little one, this is not a small stream to be crossed so easily. This is a big decision for a girl as small as you.

TONTO
Once you do this thing, you might not be able to get back.

KILLS MANY ENEMIES
Do not trust this man. Come with me. We shall ride across Mother Earth together. I will take you as my wife. You will bear me many strong children. I will call you … Stands With Short Skirt.

INJUN JOE
Hey, don't go tryin' to scare her now. She's a grown girl.

POCAHONTAS
Exactly. I am a grown girl. And it's about what he said. About doing the same thing, being trapped. I'm tired of playing in the forest. There's only so many times I can swim those stupid streams. I'm an Indian princess with no power. I mean raccoons and hummingbirds are fine, but there's got to be more to life than that. I haven't done anything substantial with my life. All I do is squeal and play like a child. It would be nice to be somebody who …

BILLY JACK
Who what …?

POCAHONTAS
Who is respected.

TONTO
Me thought you plenty respected.

POCAHONTAS
By children maybe, but realistically, what have I got to be proud of? Do you know I'm actually twelve years old?

*There is a pause as this information sinks in.*

KILLS MANY ENEMIES
You carry it well.

POCAHONTAS

I'm a twelve-year-old running around with a thirty-year-old sailor. No wonder my father wanted to kill him.

INJUN JOE

She's twelve years old? Wow. What kind of corn do your people eat?

POCAHONTAS

And let's not forget I have been with the same man for what seems like forever.

BILLY JACK

Actually more like four hundred years, if everything I suspect is true.

*There is silence.*

POCAHONTAS

I'm four hundred years old?!

TONTO

Me don't usually run into many four-hundred-year-old twelve-year-olds.

POCAHONTAS

Four hundred years old ... no wonder we have nothing left to talk about. And after all that time I invest in John, he leaves me to go back to England. Forget the little girl that gave him her heart. Typical of a man, isn't it? It's all so pointless. I have been stared at, fantasized about, romanticized, lusted after, and I have to face it all with a smile, open arms, and even open legs. The novelty has worn off. I want out!

TONTO

Now you sound plenty angry.

POCAHONTAS
    All you men are alike.

TONTO
    Hey, you barking up wrong tree.

POCAHONTAS
    (*indicating the dead white writer*) And that son of a bitch
    was going to start it all over again. Another goddamn
    story about the little lovesick Indian princess ... Damn
    it, you'd think these male writers would come up with
    an original idea once in a while instead of constantly
    putting me through this garbage. And you just reach a
    point where there have been too many broken hearts,
    too many sailors giving me the eye, too many
    conversations with raccoons, that finally something
    snaps. And you say no more. No more. The next writer
    who has me in buckskin mini-skirt, running through all
    those damned bushes knee-high in poison ivy, will be in
    deep fucking shit.

    *There is a pause of silence. POCAHONTAS realizes
    she's gone out of character and becomes embarrassed.
    She reverts to "Indian princess" mode again.*

POCAHONTAS
    Oh, I'm sorry. Must have been something I ate.

OLD LODGE SKINS
    Little one, did you kill the white man?

POCAHONTAS
    Me? No, I could never kill anybody. It just isn't in me.
    Really!

    *Everybody just stares at her. Silence.*

POCAHONTAS
Oh, come on. I was just teasing, playing. I play a lot of games where I come from.

OLD LODGE SKINS
There can be strong currents under placid waters.

INJUN JOE
So you want respect.

POCAHONTAS
Yes. I am tired of being a woman in a child's body. It might be good to bear a child, instead of being one. Can you understand?

INJUN JOE
Yes I can. The respect part, I mean.

*POCAHONTAS turns to the other characters.*

POCAHONTAS
It's not too much to ask for, is it? If that thing can do what you say.

INJUN JOE
No.

TONTO
You are right. That is not too much to ask.

INJUN JOE
You coming too?

*TONTO thinks for a moment.*

TONTO
Yes.

OLD LODGE SKINS
Another child leaves the nest.

BILLY JACK
    And you, what do you hope to find?

TONTO
    Just like young girl say, you save one white man's life,
    you stuck looking after him forever. Me like good things
    we do, but me tired of being second banana. Me want to
    wear the mask, just once. Maybe me want be … The
    Lone Indian, and he be loyal sidekick Ranger. Me like
    that. Like that a lot! Equality and freedom. That what
    me want. Dead man write more stories about more
    fights and more being faithful Indian companion. Make
    me sound like dog. Tired of same old story. No more
    hiding. No more "what we do now, Kemosabe?" Me
    want to be in charge for once. Me want to tell him and
    other people what to do. Me want be boss for once. Me
    cook for him, me do his laundry, mend bullet holes in
    his shirt. Everything. Me give him everything. And
    what me have to show for it? Nothing. And what he do
    for me? Also nothing. "Tonto, you stay here." "Tonto,
    you cover me." "Tonto, I want you to go into that
    redneck bar and start asking some questions." If me
    hear that one more time, me shoot self. If only he tell me
    he cared. Is that too much ask for? Some
    communication? After all we been through together …
    that all me ask.

INJUN JOE
    This is getting a little over my head.

KILLS MANY ENEMIES
    These are not the conversations we have on our buffalo
    hunts. Why am I vaguely uncomfortable?

TONTO
    Me know he care. Me can tell. But he cowboy in Old
    West. People there do not talk of such things. So we

must keep secret. Must it always be like this, me ask? Me want place where we can live our lives, not wear masks. Be free to love. But instead, we must always play the game, be macho, shoot big guns, get in fist fights. Live lie. Me no like live lie anymore. Me want more. Me want a real life. Me want to come out of canyon!

BILLY JACK
What are you saying?

TONTO
Nothing. Just thinking aloud. Never mind. Me talk too much.

POCAHONTAS
You didn't ... did you kill him?

TONTO
Kill who?

POCAHONTAS
The dead white writer.

TONTO
Oh no. Me good guy.

INJUN JOE
Old buddy, old pal, we'll get you a little freedom. Or die trying.

OLD LODGE SKINS
The two of you are truly brave. I envy you. I am as old as the hills, always have been, and I cannot change. I cannot even imagine the journey you attempt. Changing the world is for the young. I will stay and tend the campfire.

BILLY JACK
I will stay with you, Grandfather.

KILLS MANY ENEMIES
I will not leave your side.

OLD LODGE SKINS
Go then. Travel well. Our blessings go with you.

POCAHONTAS
I do not want to leave them. They must come with us.

TONTO
Hmm, yes. No good if left behind.

INJUN JOE
If they don't wanna go, they don't wanna go. What you gonna do? Hold a gun to their head?

*POCAHONTAS approaches the old man.*

POCAHONTAS
Yes, Grandfather, you have the wisdom of years, but please do not see that as a hindrance.

OLD LODGE SKINS
I was made old. And have always been old. That is the way of things.

POCAHONTAS
Grandfather, a twig breaks easier than a single branch; a branch breaks easier than a limb; a limb breaks easier than the trunk of a tree. And while we are on this wood metaphor, a two-hundred-year-old oak can change shape and become a fine house or a fleet of fine canoes, a totem pole even, many great things. Do not let age stop you.

*OLD LODGE SKINS takes a peek at the machine.*

OLD LODGE SKINS
It is a fine-looking machine, isn't it?

INJUN JOE

"Fine" is just a word. This thing is our dreamcatcher. It will get rid of all our bad dreams and make our good dreams come true.

OLD LODGE SKINS

Will it make me young? I want to be young.

KILLS MANY ENEMIES

But, Grandfather ... you are a grandfather. An Elder. And an Elder that is not old ... what is that?

OLD LODGE SKINS

A young man.

KILLS MANY ENEMIES

How can you want such a thing? What will happen to all your lines of wisdom? Your grey hair of understanding ... It cannot be.

OLD LODGE SKINS

My young warrior, you must understand. I've never been young like you. I've always been this age. I've never run with the buffalo like you. Or fought great battles either. I seem to have memories, but ... I remember them with my mind, not my heart. Yes, I want to be young. I want to see those battles for myself. I am tired of waiting in the teepee like a frightened old woman for the young warriors to return home with their tales of bravery. I want to be the one to come home with scalps. Can this be done?

INJUN JOE

We can find out.

*POCAHONTAS helps OLD LODGE SKINS approach the desk.*

OLD LODGE SKINS
   I thank you for giving an old man one final chance.

KILLS MANY ENEMIES
   Grandfather ...

OLD LODGE SKINS
   Yes, my son.

KILLS MANY ENEMIES
   I will join you.

TONTO
   Me confused. You just say you stay behind.

KILLS MANY ENEMIES
   With the grandfather. If he sees it best to move on, I will
   not contradict him.

BILLY JACK
   I thought you were happy with what you were.

KILLS MANY ENEMIES
   I am. I thought I was. I don't know anymore. The more
   you all talked, the more I thought. I have this long,
   unmanageable hair, and I am always ... finding things in
   it. I'm tired of it always blowing in my face; it's always
   so windy on the prairies. And those horses ... I have
   never liked horses. Nasty, brutish animals. But I must
   ride them. I would not be Kills Many Enemies if I didn't
   ride into the enemy's village on a horse. I would be
   Killed By Many Enemies. And I have no sense of
   humour. I want to be funny. I want to know irony. It is
   boring out there on the prairies, day after day, week
   after week. I mean, you gotta do something to break the
   monotony. Warriors aren't the funniest bunch of people
   to hang around with ... always trying to look and act
   macho. No. I have had enough. I want more.

INJUN JOE

That all? You want to be … funny?!

KILLS MANY ENEMIES

Yeah, and maybe a job. And short hair. And no more damned horses. And some place that's warm in the winter and cool in the summer, with lots of those cool breeze boxes over there. No bugs too. That should about cover it.

INJUN JOE

Okay, a bit specific but not unexpected.

TONTO

One left.

*They all look at BILLY JACK.*

OLD LODGE SKINS

Join an old man on his last adventure. Together we will take coup.

BILLY JACK

I have no dreams. Only reality. I've been alone before. It doesn't scare me.

OLD LODGE SKINS

You are so young to be so bitter.

BILLY JACK

I am the product of war. White man against Indians. Americans against the Vietnamese. That can make a man bitter. It would be nice to … maybe … be somebody at ease with himself. With his heritage.

POCAHONTAS

Listen, my friend. I want to leave the love that was created in me behind. I am just realizing this can be done. It is false and misplaced. Maybe you can do that with your bitterness. That is why we are going on this journey. To leave behind what we don't like about ourselves. What has wrongly been forced upon us. To be free.

BILLY JACK
You sound so sure. But without bitterness, what will I be?

POCAHONTAS
Somebody a lot less bitter. That is not so bad, is it?

KILLS MANY ENEMIES
Come with us. When we arrive … wherever we arrive, I will tell you a joke. It will make you laugh. A very hearty laugh.

BILLY JACK
(*to INJUN JOE*) Do you want me to come on your journey?

KILLS MANY ENEMIES
Not just his journey. Our journey. Your journey.

INJUN JOE
It makes no never mind to me. As long as you keep your fists to yourself.

TONTO
Me think you should come.

POCAHONTAS
Please. We started this voyage together, we should finish it together.

INJUN JOE
You afraid there, muscle boy? It could get scary.

BILLY JACK

The last time anything frightened me, I was a child.

POCAHONTAS

Maybe it's time to change that. It can be fun to be scared.

BILLY JACK

It would be nice to bring healing instead of pain. To spread knowledge instead of violence.

KILLS MANY ENEMIES

Boo! (*to TONTO*) Was that funny?

TONTO

Not really. Sorry.

*BILLY JACK thinks. He is wracked by indecision.*

BILLY JACK

(*to INJUN JOE*) Do you still think I killed the writer?

INJUN JOE

Him? It don't matter now who killed him. He's dead and we're not. (*pause*) Did you?

BILLY JACK

No. Did you?

INJUN JOE

No. It seems nobody killed the white writer, then. Bit of a mystery, huh?

BILLY JACK

Do we just leave him here?

INJUN JOE

Why not? He was going to leave us where we were. So, are you with us?

BILLY JACK
> I ... am with you.

OLD LODGE SKINS
> It is a good omen.

TONTO
> Now we can begin. What we do now ... Kemo ...

INJUN JOE
> Hey! No more of that.

> *They all crowd around the computer. INJUN JOE sits down in the chair and looks at the computer. He doesn't move.*

POCAHONTAS
> What's wrong?

INJUN JOE
> Uh, anybody know how to work this thing?

BILLY JACK
> I think so. It looks like a typewriter of some sort. Do you want me to ...

INJUN JOE
> No. Let me. I want to do it. Just ... somehow ... tell it to make me able to read and work it. Then I will take it from there.

> *BILLY JACK hesitantly taps away at the computer, writing a sentence or two. Suddenly INJUN JOE stiffens up, like he's getting an idea.*

INJUN JOE
> Gutenberg! It's all so simple. My turn! (*shifting positions with BILLY JACK*) Hallelujah! I hope everybody's been to the outhouse, 'cause we ain't stoppin' for nothing.

(*looks at writer's body*) Thanks for nothin'. Okay … here we go.

*INJUN JOE begins to type maniacally on the keyboard, laughing. And the lights start shifting around, before going down.*

*End of Act One.*

# Act Two

*Lights come up to reveal the very same office where the dead white writer had been before. Time has passed but little has changed, except the people. Their clothing, speech, and mannerisms are now contemporary. The six companions are sitting in chairs, facing each other in a circle. They look uncomfortable. Some are smoking. They make small talk amongst themselves as they wait for somebody to get things started.*

MIKE

Well, welcome, everybody, to our first meeting of the month. And wow, everybody's here today. That is truly a good omen. Glad to have you all here, together again. So who wants to start? Huh, anybody? Floor's open.

*Again another uncomfortable pause. Finally BILL takes a deep breath, and stands up.*

BILL

All right, I'll get this freak show started. Hi, my name is Bill, and I'm an alcoholic.

EVERYBODY

Hello, Bill.

BILL

I haven't drank in, oh I guess a coupla months now. I guess that's pretty good, huh?

*They all applaud him.*

MIKE

And why did you drink, Bill?

BILL

Hell, for the simplest reason in the world …

JIM

A woman?

BILL

Hell no. Women are hardly simple, trust me. I drank to get drunk. Next question.

MIKE

Bill, why did you want to get drunk? There's gotta be a deeper reason.

BILL

Pressure, I guess. You see, I'm under a hell of a lot of pressure at work. As you know, I run the Flaming Arrow Casino …

SALLY

Yeah, the one out by Highway 73. That's a nice place.

BILL

Thanks. Wait till you see the renovations. The biggest air conditioning system in the province. And picture a huge medicine wheel over the roof of the casino, with all the lines made by laser beams.

JOHN

Isn't that kinda sacrilegious?

BILL

Hell no. It's all good. We got a write-up in *Architecture Today*. The style is called Nouveau Native. We even had the whole placed blessed by Mike here. Eh, Mike?

MIKE

Yeah, it took 143 braids of sweetgrass to smudge the place. That's one big casino.

BILL

You know what they say … size matters.

*He waits for a laugh that doesn't come.*

SALLY

Do you got bingo?

BILL

Bingo?! No, I don't "got" bingo. That's so rez.

FRED

Rez …? Res … residential school? Are you talking about residential schools? I went to one of those. I remember …

MIKE

We know, Fred. That's why you're here.

FRED

That's why I'm here.

JOHN

You started drinking because of it.

FRED

I drink because of it.

MIKE

But not anymore.

FRED

But not anymore. That's why I'm here.

*FRED starts to cry.*

BILL

Oh man, he's starting to cry again. I hate it when he does this.

SALLY

Leave him alone.

MIKE

Fred. It's okay. It's me. Did you have another flashback?

FRED

They don't go away. The memories. I can still see them. Smell them. It hurts, Mike. It hurts. Are you sure I don't drink anymore? I sure could use one. It makes them go away.

MIKE

That doesn't help, Fred. It only makes things worse. That's why we're all here. To support each other. Your friends are a much better crutch to lean on than drinking.

JIM

Me, I'm here for the donuts.

SALLY

Shut up, Jim.

MIKE

Fred, you know I'm your friend, right?

FRED

Yes. You're my friend.

MIKE

I'm the one who helped you, remember? I got you into that treatment centre. The one I stayed at. I became your sponsor. I drive you here for every meeting. I take you to the sweats, Fred. I'm your friend and I wouldn't lie to you. Okay?

SALLY

You listen to Mike, Fred. He knows what he's talking about.

FRED

My friends ... you guys are my friends aren't you?

BILL

You bet.

JOHN

"All for one" and all that sort of stuff.

FRED

We've always been friends, haven't we?

MIKE

I guess you could say that. Ever since the beginning. Come on, let's take our seats again.

SALLY

Bill, if we can, I want to get back to the bingo issue ...

BILL

Nobody plays bingo anymore, Sally. Get with the times. We got blackjack, keno, slot machines, roulette, craps, baccarat, and a half-dozen other games from around the world that you ain't never heard of ...

SALLY

No bingo ... Now *that's* sacrilegious!

MIKE

People, we seem to be getting a little off topic here. Bill, you were telling us about how you became an alcoholic.

JIM

Oh, who cares anymore?

JOHN

I care. He is our brother. He must be supported.

BILL

Thanks, John. Like I said, it was the casino. Way too much pressure. Way too many decisions. Drinking helped me not get so nervous and frustrated. I discovered owning your own liquor licence is a mixed blessing. Man, if this thing goes down the tubes, it's over for me.

MIKE

Positive thinking, Bill. And how's the family?

BILL

Jill's living up north, with the kids. I miss them.

SALLY

Maybe they'll come back. Once they see how well you're doing.

BILL

Sally, you were always the optimist of the group. I think that's why I'm working so hard on the casino. I don't want to think about Jill and the kids, or how badly I want a drink. The more I concentrate on the casino, the less time I have to worry about anything else. (*to JOHN*) Oh, John, by the way, did you bring my cigarettes with you when you came down?

JOHN

Yep, ninety-four boxes in my trunk, but we'll do business later.

JIM

Can we speed this up?

SALLY

What's your hurry?

JIM

I got things to do. Important things.

SALLY

Speaking of important things, Chief Jim, when do we get our welfare cheques?

JIM

They're in the mail.

SALLY

What mail? You live half a kilometre down the road. In your new house. The band office is a kilometre in the other direction. And who ever heard of a band office with a hot tub? It's easier and quicker if I come up tomorrow and pick it up directly.

JIM

You can do whatever the hell you want, but it's still going to be in the mail.

MIKE

Now, Jim …

JIM

Look, Mike, I never wanted to be a part of this stupid circle. I don't have a drinking problem.

MIKE

We've all heard that before.

JIM

A couple glasses of wine isn't worth all this shit.

JOHN

Then why are you here?

*For a moment, JIM looks uncomfortable.*

JIM

Because ... because you guys are all here.

MIKE

Do you hate being alone, Jim?

JIM

I get nervous sometimes ... it's like somebody's watching me. Us. Something like that.

JOHN

And people call me paranoid.

BILL

Well, if you'd stop blockading the Tim Hortons, people might like you more.

JOHN

Hey, that's a righteous political act that demonstrates our sovereignty against a symbol of Canadian imperialism.

BILL

For God's sake, it's owned by that Wendy's hamburger chain. In the States. Do your research, John.

JIM

Seriously, people. I haven't felt right in a long time.

FRED

Me either.

JIM

For some reason ... somehow ... I feel safer with you guys. I don't know why, but ...

MIKE

Jim, are you reaching out to us?!

SALLY

I think he is.

JIM

Oh, go to hell.

MIKE

No, no. Jim. Stay with us. Let's explore this feeling. Is this why you embezzled that money from the Department of Indian Affairs, and the band office, and those other two businesses ... for a sense of security if something goes wrong? A nest egg? It's quite common, you know.

JIM

I didn't steal any money. That's not been proven.

SALLY

Yet ...

JIM

Ah, fuck you all. I should have kept my mouth shut.

FRED

I'm tired.

JIM

So am I. Of this whole fucking arrangement.

SALLY

Why are you tired, Fred?

FRED

I just am. I wanna go home. (*pause*) Hey, this place looks familiar.

*They all go silent.*

FRED

Were we here before?

SALLY

Fred, honey, don't you remember?

FRED

I think I remember somebody ... somebody died. A white guy. Yeah. Over there. Wasn't there a dead white guy over there ... once?

SALLY

Yes, Fred, once—but remember we promised never to say anything about him ever again?

FRED

We did? Why?

SALLY

Just because, Fred. Just because.

FRED

I guess that's a good reason.

JIM

He's fried. Man, I thought I was bad off, but he's tobogganning down a steep hill with no toboggan. Or snow.

FRED

Where is he?

SALLY

Who, Fred?

FRED

The dead white … writer. That's it. He was a writer. He wrote things. Didn't he?

JOHN

Fred, just let it go. That was a long time ago.

FRED

No it wasn't.

BILL

Will somebody shut him up?

MIKE

Fred, why don't you tell us about why you're here?

FRED

I'm here because I wanted to be here. Didn't we all want to be here? We all brought ourselves here. Didn't we?

MIKE

No, Fred. Why you're here at this A.A. meeting. What made you start drinking?

FRED

'Cause I'm a drunk.

JOHN

Christ, Oka didn't take this long.

MIKE

Fred, pay attention. Why are you a drunk? What made you a drunk? And what made you stop?

FRED

Oh, what made me a drunk. (*pause*) I think it was the drinking.

JIM

Jesus!

FRED

I went to residential school. Did I ever tell you what happened there?

JIM

Every friggin' meeting. Mike …

MIKE

Cut him some slack, Jim. You know what he's been through. He's had it rougher than any of us.

JOHN

But he wanted to be educated. It's not our fault. And he keeps breaking our agreement.

SALLY

He's ill. Aren't you, sweetie?

FRED

I'm ill.

JOHN

We're all ill, Sally. It's an A.A. meeting, for Christ's sake. But there are rules. We agreed. He agreed. We can't break the rules.

FRED

I know. I'm bad. Did I tell you I saw him?

MIKE

Saw who?

FRED

The dead writer guy.

*Everybody freezes.*

FRED

Except he wasn't dead. Unless dead people work at the liquor store. He's back from the dead. And he wasn't writing. He sold me a mickey of vodka, just a little while ago. He had a nice smile.

*Everybody is silent as what FRED says sinks in.*

JIM

That's impossible.

FRED

No, his smile was very nice.

JIM

Fuck, he's hallucinating again. We should have left him in the rehab centre.

FRED

Where did we last put him?

SALLY

Who, honey?

FRED

The dead white writer. Where'd we leave him ... I think it was over there, wasn't it?

JOHN

Mike, he's going out of character. Do something!

JIM

Shut up, Fred.

MIKE

Leave him alone. Fred, there is no more dead white writer. You must have seen somebody else that just looked like him. He's gone.

FRED

Gone? How can he be gone? People can't just be gone.

BILL

Yes, they can be gone. We got rid of him. And we
promised we'd never mention him again. So don't.

JOHN

Yeah.

FRED

Did we ever find out who killed him?

*Everybody is silent.*

JIM

Fred … sit down and shut up before I knock you back to
the 1800s.

*FRED gets up and wanders over to the place where
the dead white writer used to be.*

FRED

We left him over here, didn't we?

JIM

Fred, what part of "sit down and shut up" didn't you
understand?

JOHN

I thought we were having an A.A. meeting. What
happened to that? Hi, my name is John and I'm an …

JIM

Ah, Christ, give it up and let's go home. I never should
have come back here. Anybody need a ride? I brought
my Hummer.

BILL

You got a Hummer? Man, don't those things cost a fortune?

SALLY

On a chief's salary?

JIM

I shop a lot in dollar stores. Leave me alone.

JOHN

Hey, wait a minute. I didn't get a chance to finish. I'm just as much an alcoholic as you guys.

MIKE

John, please …

JOHN

Mike, Mike, please, let me talk. Okay. I just need a few minutes.

MIKE

It's fine with me. If it's fine with everybody else?

SALLY/BILL/JIM

Yeah, sure, what the hell.

MIKE

Go ahead, John.

JOHN

Hi, my name is John and I'm an alcoholic.

EVERYBODY

(*unenthusiastically*) Hello, John.

JOHN

Um, yeah, I've been sober for almost two months now. Power to the people. Thank you.

JIM

That's it?

JOHN

I didn't say I'd be long.

JIM

I think your bone choker's on a little too tight.

MIKE

John, what made you start to drink?

JOHN

Oh, I never actually drank. Never touch the stuff.

BILL

Then why the hell are you here?

JOHN

I just want to hang out. It's a slow week, protest-wise.

BILL

I'm tellin' you, man, that Federation of Warriors thing you tried to put together, that was funny.

JOHN

It was not.

BILL

Yeah, what did you originally call it?

JIM

Oh yeah, the Canadian Organization of Warrior Societies.

BILL

Or C.O.W.S. for short. You lost a lot of credibility for that one, my friend. Acronyms, always have somebody check your acronyms.

JOHN

Bill, you know as well as I do, we're not called that anymore. We're the Warrior Alliance of Canada.

BILL

Yeah, that's much better. W.A.C. John, my friend, you are truly whacked.

SALLY

Fred, what are you doing?

*FRED walks up to the closet door and tries to open it. It is locked. He keeps trying.*

MIKE

Fred, it's locked. It won't open.

FRED

I think we put him in here. Didn't we? Didn't we put him in here? 'Cause that's where we found him. We put him back where we found him. We were very neat.

JIM

Ah, man, there he goes again. I thought we put all this behind us.

FRED

(*pointing to MIKE*) And you have the key.

JOHN

Mike, how does he know that?

SALLY

Do you have the key?

JIM

I thought you said you threw it away.

*They all look expectantly at MIKE.*

JIM

Well, Mike? Do you still have the key?

*MIKE seems a little defensive. He shuffles uncomfortably before reaching into his shirt pocket and pulling out a small key.*

BILL

Oh, man … Why, Mike?

MIKE

I was going to throw it away after Jim did … what Jim said he was going to do. But still, I consider it a symbol of our journey from chaos to reality, a talisman on our path to wellness. Besides, it's all we have left.

JOHN

We didn't want anything left. That's why we left. You agreed.

SALLY

You did agree, Mike. We all heard you.

BILL

This is all a crock of shit! I can't believe we're back talking about this again. He was gone. We were free.

FRED

Can I have the key, please?

MIKE

You don't want the key, Fred.

JOHN

None of us wants that damned key.

SALLY

Fred, honey, why do you want the key?

FRED

I want to see him.

SALLY

Why?

FRED

Something's different.

MIKE

A lot's different, Fred. Why look at him now?

FRED

That's why all of us showed up for today's meeting. Something's not right.

BILL

Oh, for the love of … I'm telling you, man. He's wandering through the forest without a compass. (*yelling*) What's not right, ya crazy …?

FRED

Us. We're not right. You felt it, didn't you?

JIM

I didn't feel anything. I take it all back. Everything's fine.

BILL

Fred, you're not right in the head. Everybody knows that. But don't drag us on your little vision quest. I'm just peachy. Fuckin' fine.

JOHN

Me too.

JIM

I'm finer than fine.

FRED

Please, Mike, give me the key. I have to see him.

JIM/JOHN/BILL/SALLY

Don't do it. This isn't right. Just throw it away.

*There is a moment of silence.*

MIKE

It's just a key.

FRED

It's just a key.

*He takes it from MIKE and opens the door. Once
again we can see only the legs of the dead white writer.
The rest of him is obscured.*

JIM

Shit.

SALLY

There he is.

BILL

Close the door.

FRED

I remember now.

BILL

Mike, close the damned door.

*MIKE closes it. There is silence.*

JOHN

That was a stupid thing to do.

BILL

(*to JIM*) I thought you were gonna get rid of him.

JIM

I … I never got around to it.

BILL

You never got around to it! How can you not get around
to disposing of a dead body?! That's kind of high on
most politicians' priority lists.

JIM

Hey, I'm a busy guy. I got a reserve to run.

BILL

I think I liked you better when you could barely talk.
Well, how long were you gonna let him stay in there?
I'm surprised he ain't smelling up the place. If
somebody finds him, this will be really bad for business.

JIM

Well, if you're in such a damned hurry to get rid of him,
be my guest.

BILL

It wasn't my responsibility. Mike, Jim, you had the key.
You two were responsible for taking care of … this.
Don't shove it off on us.

MIKE

I thought he took care of it. Honest. I even said a
blessing over him. I mean … we don't have to be
savages.

JIM

I have my own key.

MIKE

You do? When? Why?

JIM

Because I wanted to. I have the keys to every place in this community.

MIKE

Where is it now?

JIM

In the glove compartment of my Hummer.

BILL

You had your own key and you "never got around to it"? How irresponsible.

JIM

Excuse me, but do you know how many things I'm juggling at the moment?! I don't have a lot of time. I got other priorities.

SALLY

Like sending out our welfare cheques?! I'm serious about this, Jim. My kids gotta eat. You know as well as I do that little Frank is way too small for his age. He's gotta eat more. And little Angie still has that sore throat. And when's the housing repair committee going to come and take a look at my house? I got drafts coming through holes in my walls that are bigger than hummingbirds and raccoons. Huh? When?

JIM

Talk to the band council. I don't care about your drafts and snot-nosed kids. There are bigger issues here.

SALLY

Honey, there's nothing bigger or more important than my kids. Listen here, I'm coming up to that office first thing tomorrow, and my cheque better be there or you're going to get one size-six shoe up your ass.

JIM

Honey, you ain't been a size-six anything since we got
here and you discovered Indian tacos. And I've had
bigger and badder women try to do me harm. You're
just another face in this crowd of ingrates.

FRED

You saw him, too, didn't you?

JIM

Saw who? No, I didn't. I didn't see anybody. You're one
crazy loon.

FRED

That's why you didn't move his body. It freaked you
out. That's why you're here. Where did you see him?

*Everybody looks at JIM. He looks cornered.*

MIKE

Jim?

JIM

Oh, relax. It wasn't him. Just another good-looking
white guy, with a strong chin. I got ... friends that do
stuff. Stuff that sometimes needs to be done. Handle ...
things discreetly, if you know what I mean.

SALLY

Ho-ly, everything we've heard about you ... it's true.

JIM

No, it's not. I categorically deny it. And I'm innocent till
proven guilty. Still, I thought it best to call this guy
about moving the body, and he and some muscle
showed up to negotiate ... and ...

SALLY

And ...

JIM

> The guy with the pickaxe ... in the right light, from the right angle, without the beard ... you could almost swear ...

JOHN

> Shit, what does that mean?

JIM

> Nothing. It means nothing. I said it wasn't him. It just looked like him. No need to freak out.

MIKE

> Everybody, just calm down. Sally, calm down. You too, Jim. I'm sure you're right. It couldn't have been him. He's right here. But Bill's right too. We can't just leave the body in there. We've got to do something.

BILL

> Wow, Mike, you hold one hell of an A.A. meeting. Few more of these and I'll want to start drinking again.

FRED

> It's not right.

SALLY

> Honey, you said that before. Everything's just fine. We're just having some disagreements. Honestly. Why don't you just sit down and rest a while? Here, have some coffee. It will calm you down.

JIM

> I could just kick his ass. He's ruining everything.

MIKE

> (*indicating the body*) Still, back to the main argument, are you gonna eventually do something about ... him?

JIM

Yeah, it's on my list of things to do. Tomorrow. I'll take care of it tomorrow. I've got these other friends …

BILL

You and your friends … do any of them wear a mask?

JIM

Bill, don't push me. Just because you financed my campaign, don't mean …

BILL

Don't mean what?

FRED

(*to SALLY*) Are you happy?

SALLY

Am I happy? What do you mean?

FRED

(*to MIKE*) Mike, are you happy? Are you the man you wanted to be?

JIM

Don't answer him. He's off again.

FRED

(*to JIM*) What about you?

JIM

I'm not talking to you.

FRED

This isn't me. This isn't you.

JOHN

Maybe we should consider getting him to a hospital or something. He could be having a stroke or something.

*FRED gets up quickly and opens the door again, to look at the body.*

BILL
He's at it again. Fred, sit down. The writer's not going anywhere.

JOHN
Maybe you should lock him back in the closet again. Till, like, you actually get rid of him. I'd feel safer.

*FRED kneels down and touches the body. SALLY tries to lead him away.*

SALLY
Fred, leave the man alone. Come with me and …

FRED
I thought you said he was dead.

SALLY
He is.

FRED
Then why is he warm?

BILL
Warm?! Who? The writer?

JIM
Impossible. He's dead.

*SALLY reaches in and hesitantly touches the body. She quickly removes her hand, frightened.*

SALLY
He's right. He's warm. I think I felt a pulse. Ho-ly, he is alive!

JOHN

He can't be. He's been in there for …

*JOHN rushes in between them, roughly pushing
FRED aside. Almost immediately, he stumbles back,
away from the body.*

JOHN

JESUS MOTHER OF GOD!

SALLY

I told you. I told you!

JIM

It's a trick. A trick Fred's playing on us.

JOHN

No! He is alive. He is! It was him. I knew it was him.

*One by one, they all turn to look at JOHN, who is
getting more and more frantic.*

MIKE

John …?

JOHN

He was the cop! It was hard to tell behind the shades,
but I knew, I could tell, I just didn't want to admit it.

FRED

John sees. John knows.

JOHN

I got … I got … I got pulled over a while back. For
smuggling cigarettes, you know, to finance the cause …
it's hard to change the world on just pocket change …
and I got pulled over. I was in the process of calling my
lawyer, and my publicist, when the cop stepped up to
my window. I couldn't speak or anything. I mean, this

had happened a dozen times before, and if nothing else, it was good publicity for the cause. But this time he took all my product ... I let him, and then I sat there on the side of the road, for an hour. Trying to tell myself that wasn't him. But it must have been.

BILL

It wasn't. You're all suffering from some sort of post-traumatic stress thing. That's got to be the answer. We're looking at his fucking body.

*They all crowd around the doorway, getting in each other's way.*

MIKE

Everybody, just step back. Let's ... let's just figure this out. Okay?

*They all step back. MIKE closes the closet door. Silence. More silence.*

MIKE

Anybody got any ideas?

JIM

Maybe he wasn't dead to begin with.

BILL

No, he was dead. I'd stake everything I know for a fact he was dead. You forget, I know dead. In another time I'd sliced, chopped, and filleted enough people to open a alternative sushi bar. But if he wasn't actually ... really dead, what has he been doing in there all this time ... hibernating?

SALLY

Fred, do you know what's going on?

JIM

Why are you asking him? He's a basket case.

SALLY

It all started with him.

JOHN

She's right. It did.

SALLY

Fred, honey …

FRED

It didn't work out.

BILL

What didn't work out? What's he talking about?

FRED

I didn't want to be … this. What I am.

JIM

I don't blame you. I wouldn't want to be you either.

FRED

I just wanted some education. To be smarter and more like them and less like I was. But not this. I became this.

JIM

Yeah, your life's pathetic, but what's that got to do with us?

FRED

It's the same with you. You're going to jail.

JIM

I am not!

FRED

You used to send people to jail, remember? (*to JOHN*)
And you ... you smuggle cigarettes. (*to BILL*) You are
building an altar to aboriginal capitalism. (*to SALLY*)
You spend all your free time playing a game to provide
for your kids. (*to MIKE*) And you get paid by the hour
to be native. This isn't what we planned. Don't you
think there's something wrong with all this?

JIM

I think there's something wrong with you.

FRED

We started down the same road, but ended up on these
side streets. This isn't the destination we ...

MIKE

Everybody, just calm down. Maybe we need a smudge.

BILL

Oh, smudge this, you sanctimonious cretin. How's that
for education?

JOHN

I can't believe he's still alive. I can't believe it. I don't
understand it. What do we do now?

BILL

John, you're giving me a headache.

JOHN

I'm giving you a headache! You! My heart's beating like
a fucking rabbit and you're worried about your
goddamned headache. He's alive in there! Haven't you
heard anything?
(*at the closet*) Why can't you stay dead?!

BILL

Not very warrior of you.

JOHN

Shut up! Shut up! Shut up!

BILL

Looks to me like you could use one of those cigarettes you've been hauling.

*JOHN angrily jumps on BILL and they fall to the ground. SALLY and MIKE race in to separate them.*

JIM

It's a good thing you don't charge for these A.A. meetings, Mike.

MIKE

Stop it, all of you! Quit acting like this is a band council meeting.

FRED

I wanna go back.

SALLY

Back to what?

FRED

I don't like the way I am. I want to go back. To the way I was before. This was all a mistake.

BILL

Did he say he wants to go back? Ah, fuck! We shouldn't have brought him. We should have kept him locked up somewhere.

SALLY

We can't go back, Fred. We all made a promise. Remember? New lives, new everything.

FRED

There were a lot of promises. We didn't like the way we were before, so we changed everything. I don't like the way things are now … so I want to change it. What's changed from before?

JOHN

Fred, Fred, Fred, yeah, I know your life isn't what you expected. Mine isn't either. Look at me; it's the middle of winter and I'm wearing summer camouflage. Some things don't make sense because they just don't. You just have to accept it. Fred, do you like me? Am I your friend?

FRED

Yes, John. You are.

JOHN

So stop this silly talk and let's get on with the meeting. Okay, buddy? Maybe if we just ignore everything, pretended …

FRED

John, I'm sorry. I seem to have made you think I'm in control here. I'm not. I'm just along for the ride, like the rest of you. I'm just not happy about it. That's all.

JOHN

Fred, I've made a life for myself here. Yeah, it's not what I expected. But that's part of life. Nobody ever gets the life they expected. We were bored and unhappy before. I'm not bored or unhappy anymore. And I'm young and actually doing things. That's a good thing, don't you think?

FRED

Not for me.

JOHN

(*yelling*) There's more to this than just you, GODDAMNIT! There's Bill and his dream casino, Sally and her kids. Mike has that lecture tour of Germany coming up. We all have dreams. Nobody has the right to take them away. Just because your life is shitty ...

FRED

These aren't dreams. These are nightmares. Sally, you wanted to have children instead of being one. Now, you have almost a dozen with no way of supporting them. Was that your dream?

SALLY

No. It just sort of ... happened. I just wanted to become a real woman. There's nothing wrong with that.

MIKE

Fred, we made due. We made our choices. Life happens. Things change. Like John said, we adapted. Indigenous people in general are very adaptable. Look at the Inuit, they ...

JIM

Fuck the Inuit.

FRED

Maybe the writer had dreams too. Before one of us killed him. Or didn't kill him.

JOHN

Will somebody shut him up!

MIKE

Fred, I know it's hard, but try to remember. We all promised each other that we'd look after each other. That we'd search for a new life. Together. That's why we're here. You must remember that.

FRED

But this isn't any better. In fact, we made it worse. We made ourselves. At least we used to have the luxury of blaming him. We don't have that luxury anymore.

BILL

Geez, that almost makes sense.

SALLY

No it doesn't. I will not go back to what I was. I love my kids, Fred. I won't leave them.

FRED

How many kids do you have?

SALLY

What does that have to do with anything?

FRED

You have eleven kids, don't you, with four different fathers—Mike being one of them. You're on welfare, a quarter of which goes to playing bingo. You're smoking yourself to death on the cigarettes John supplies to Bill's casino and Jim's store. You're thirty pounds overweight …

SALLY

So I'm not perfect. Neither are you.

FRED

I know. I wasn't perfect before either. But at least I didn't have these memories. Or what's left of my liver. Given a choice—and we had one once—I'd return to what I was. I have to. Otherwise, I'll die like this.

JIM

Then die. You can't handle it here … fine. We can. I like being the boss, so die and be done with it.

FRED

Sorry, it's not my choice.

*SALLY breathes in audibly, in shock.*

MIKE

Sally, what's wrong?

SALLY

That's what he said! "Sorry, it's not my choice." Those
were his words!

MIKE

Whose words? Sally, what are you talking about?

JOHN

You know what she's talking about. (*quickly*) Fuck. Fuck.
Fuck. Fuck.

BILL

Not her too.

SALLY

I knew I'd seen him somewhere before, but I'd just come
home from a "Midnight to Dawn Bingo Blowout" and
was very tired. Everything was blurry and hazy. He'd
come to the house, early in the morning. He'd heard
some disquieting things about how I was raising my
kids. Wanted to investigate. He was from the Children's
Aid Society. I asked him to leave us alone—what did we
ever do to him? And he said, "It's not my choice." He
said he'd come back … tomorrow. "Sorry, it's not my
choice." That's what he said.

JOHN

Oh shit!

FRED

Bill?

BILL

What?

FRED

You've seen him too, haven't you? Somewhere, alive.

*BILL is silent.*

JIM

Bill?

BILL

I think he's the contractor for the casino renovations.

JOHN

We're screwed. We're screwed. We're screwed.

SALLY

That leaves you, Mike.

MIKE

(*pause*) At one of the ceremonies I officiated at, I was given, as a gift, an Iroquois false face. I think his face was on it … a little distorted, but yeah. It was him. I am almost sure. (*pause*) I'm … afraid.

BILL

It doesn't matter. None of this matters. We're here, and nothing is going to change. I'm not going anywhere.

FRED

But nothing has changed, Bill. That's it. We exchanged one pair of moccasins for another. Things didn't get better.

BILL

The hell they didn't. I'm rich.

FRED

At everybody's expense.

JIM

I run this reserve. I'm respected. I am in charge.

FRED

Actually, you're not for much longer. And you've got nobody to save you this time. Nobody's arriving in the nick of time.

MIKE

Is it just me or is Fred sounding awfully … coherent, all of a sudden? Twenty minutes ago he couldn't tie his shoes. Now he …

JOHN

What have you done, you son of a bitch?

FRED

I didn't do anything. We didn't do anything.

JOHN

Fuck you and fuck this fucking weird white guy. I'm getting the hell out of here.

*JOHN runs to the exit, but it is locked. He cannot open it.*

JOHN

It's locked. It can't be locked. We never lock it. Why is this door locked? Mike, why is this door locked?

*MIKE tries the door, and indeed, it is locked.*

MIKE

It is locked. This is not good.

JOHN

Oh shit! Oh shit! My heart's beating like a rabbit again.

BILL

Oh, you and your rabbits.

SALLY

Fred, did you lock the door?

FRED

I never touched the door.

SALLY

Then how did it get locked?

FRED

Sally, honey, it was never opened.

JIM

What the hell is he talking about? We all walked in here not more than an hour ago. Outside that door are all our cars and our new lives. He's more screwed up than we thought.

FRED

I'll be glad to go back.

BILL

Why?

FRED

I'd rather live in somebody else's hell than my own. John, Sally, Jim, Bill, Mike, we are who we are, no matter what we do. I know you'd all like to blame the writer, but ...

MIKE

Then ... who is he, the writer?

FRED

(*with a slight Missouri accent*) Well, that's for somebody a lot smarter than me to answer.

JOHN

Yeah, well, we're not going back. At least I'm not. I won't be old again. I like my teeth.

FRED

It's not that easy.

SALLY

What do you know that we don't?

*FRED shrugs his shoulders.*

BILL

There's got to be an answer to all this.

JOHN

I don't wanna go back. I don't wanna.

SALLY

Fred, you're scaring John.

FRED

No, John is scaring John. I keep telling you, this is not my doing.

JOHN

Mike, do something.

MIKE

Maybe a sweat might help.

JIM

I think John's sweating enough already.

MIKE

Listen, everybody. We're all still in control. Nobody panic. Now, Fred … brother Fred. You're making this all up, aren't you? You're playing the trickster on us, huh? Just a little bit?

FRED

No, Mike. You wanted to heal instead of hurt people.
Everybody here is hurting in some way. This is how we
heal.

JOHN

No, no, no! I don't care what Fred says. He has to be
wrong. I'm positive the writer is behind this, somehow.
Maybe ... maybe ... if we kill the dead white writer
again, and then get rid of his body for sure this time,
everything will be okay. Maybe he'll disappear again.
He did for a while. What do you think?

BILL

Kill him again? How many times does one of us have to
kill him?

JIM

Sounds like a plan. Well, who killed him last time?

*There is silence. They all glance at each other,*
*expecting a response or confession.*

JIM

Oh, Jesus Christ, not this again. Look, one of you killed
him. There's been a lot of water under the bridge since
then, and it would save us an awful lot of time and
headaches if whoever did it in the first place would
stand up and confess.

*They stand waiting again.*

JIM

Oh, for the love of ... come on, let's all do it.

*He pushes past everyone and walks toward the closet.*
*He throws open the door and freezes.*

JIM

You have got to be fucking kidding me!

BILL

What?!

JIM

He's gone.

*JIM steps away from the doorway, revealing an empty closet. The body has disappeared.*

JOHN

Fuck! Fuck! Fuck! Oh fuck!

SALLY

Where is he?

BILL

Maybe he's hiding. If he's still alive, could he be hiding? Huh? Do you think?

*JIM kicks the walls of the closet. They all seem solid.*

JIM

Where the hell is he gonna hide?

BILL

He must have gone somewhere.

JIM

Obviously—but where?

SALLY

There's no other way out of here.

FRED

I know.

JIM

"I know." What the hell do you know? Tell us what's happening.

FRED

You know that sense of paranoia you told us about earlier?

JIM

Yeah ...

FRED

You're a lot more perceptive than you realize.

MIKE

Fred, where is the writer? What happened to him?

FRED

Honestly, I don't know. This is all new to me too.

MIKE

But you're the only one who seems to know what's going on ... or you're the least surprised.

FRED

Well, fatalism has its benefits.

JOHN

(*to the room*) I can be a better person. I just want the chance. I tried to be a warrior for the best causes. I did! (*yells out*) Hey, don't do this. I want another chance. I mean, this was our first time. Everybody gets a second chance, don't they? Practice makes perfect, right?

JIM

For God's sake, have some dignity.

BILL

I wanted to open my new casino. That's not so bad, is it?
All the money was going to the community ... most of
it. What's wrong with building a dream? Of creating a
future for my people. Sally, you could've worked there.
Really. I'd hire you in a second.

SALLY

You would? I'd have a job!

BILL

Yeah. We'd even provide day care.

SALLY

Now you tell me. That would have been so nice ...
maybe we can still ... hey, it's getting dark.

BILL

(*looks out the window*) It can't be getting dark. It's still
early.

SALLY

No, dark in here.

JIM

Hey, she's right.

*They look around and, indeed, the room seems to be
getting darker. Around the edge of the room, the lights
are getting dimmer, like an iris closing.*

MIKE

That's odd. What would cause that?

BILL

Maybe it's an eclipse?

SALLY

Inside?

*JOHN tries turning on the lamp, with little effect. He tries to turn on all the lights, again with little success.*

JOHN
Something's wrong, man.

FRED
It's over, I guess.

JOHN
What's over?

FRED
The A.A. meeting. Us. All of this.

JIM
It can't be. I won't let it.

FRED
There's nothing you can do.

JIM
I am a man. I exist. I have a life. I can do something. I have a right to determine my own life, damn it!

FRED
I can feel it already. Can you?

*JIM does indeed feel something. So does everybody else. They are unnerved by it.*

JIM
Fred, help me, please.

FRED
I tried. We all tried.

SALLY
I ... I think it's growing. The darkness. Look!

*They watch as the darkness at the edge of the room continues to expand toward them. The companions start to huddle around the centre of the room.*

JOHN
Fred, make it stop.

FRED
I wouldn't if I could. It's time to go.

SALLY
Where?

FRED
I guess ... home ...

JOHN
Home ...

BILL
Home ...

FRED
Home.

*They huddle closer to the desk at centre stage, as the darkness begins to creep even closer.*

MIKE
I guess nobody killed the dead white writer then.

FRED
It was never about him.

MIKE
Then this was all for nothing.

JIM
Me was so close to making it. To getting away.

FRED

No, Jim, you weren't.

BILL

What happens now?

JOHN

Yeah, what?

FRED

We'll find out.

SALLY

But it's not fair.

FRED

No, Sally, it's not.

BILL

I ... I did not even get a chance to be funny.

*Fade to black.*

*End.*

# Stories We Listened To

# Stories We Listened To
## J O H N   H A I N E S

The Bench Press / SWARTHMORE / PENNSYLVANIA

Copyright © 1986 by John Haines

The Bench Press
408 Haverford Place
Swarthmore, Pennsylvania 19081

Printed in the United States of America
90  89  88  87      5  4  3  2

These essays appeared previously in the following publications:
*Antaeus* Spring/Summer, 1982: "Out of the Shadows"; *The Daily
News,* Anchorage, Alaska, June, 1982: "Burning a Porcupine";
*Kansas Quarterly,* Spring, 1982: "Ice"; *New England Review,*
Summer, 1983: "Death Is a Meadowlark" and Winter, 1983:
"Stories We Listened To." Earlier versions of them also appeared
in *The Homer News* and *Nature Conservancy News.*

Library of Congress Cataloging-in-Publication Data

Haines, John Meade, 1924–
      Stories we listened to.

      Contents: Introduction—Stories we listened to—
Out of the shadows—[etc.]
      I. Title.
PS3558.A33S86   1985      813'.54        85-22948
ISBN 0-930769-02-3 cloth
ISBN 0-930769-01-5 paper

Photograph by William Stafford looking south from
John Haines' homestead, milepost 68 outside
Fairbanks, Alaska, 1976.

for Jo Marian Going

# Contents

# Prologue

---

THERE ARE SHADOWS *over the land. They come out of the ground, from the dust and the tumbled bones of the earth. Tree shadows that haunt the woodlands of childhood, holding fear in their branches. Stone shadows on the desert, cloud shadows on the sea and over the summer hills, bringing water. Shapes of shadow in pools and wells, vague forms in the sandlight.*

*Out of the past come these wind-figures, the flapping sails of primitive birds with terrible beaks and claws. Shadows of things that walked once and went away. Lickers of blood that fasten by night to the veins of standing cattle, to the foot of a sleeping man. In the Far North the heavy, stalled bodies of mastodons chilled in a black ooze, and their fur-clad bones still come out of the ground. Triceratops was feeding in the marshlands, by the verge of the coal-making forests.*

*Shadows in doorways, and under the eaves of ancient buildings, where the fallen creatures of stone grimace in sleep. Domestic, wind-tugged shadows cast by icy branches upon a bedroom window: they tap on the glass and wake us. They speak to the shadows within us, old ghosts that will not die. Like trapped, primordial birds, they break from an ice-pool in the heart's well and fly into walls built long ago.*

*Stand still where you are—at the end of pavement, in a sun-break of the forest, on the open, cloud-peopled terrace of the plains. Look deeply into the wind-furrows of the grass, into the leaf-stilled water of pools.*

1

# Prologue

*Think back through the silence, of the life that was and is not here now, of the strong pastness of things—shadows of the end and the beginning.*

*It is autumn. Leaves are flying, a storm of them over the land. They are brown and yellow, parched and pale—Shelly's "pestilence-stricken multitudes." Out of an evening darkness they fly in our faces and scare us; like resigned spirits they whirl away and spill into hollows, to lie still, one on the other, waiting for snow.*

# Stories We Listened To

———

IT IS EVENING in the kitchen of the roadhouse at Richardson, past dusk of a winter day. A gas lantern is burning overhead, throwing strong light on the white enamel of the shelves and cupboards, a brightness on the hanging pots and pans. A white oilcloth marked with a well-rubbed floral pattern gleams on the long table in the center of the room.

Three of us are sitting at the table—Allison, Melvin and myself—drinking coffee laced with strong rum. A heated and windy sigh comes from the flue of the Great Majestic range standing black and heavy at one end of the room.

Allison is speaking, relaxed at the end of a day of roadhouse chores. His favorite black chauffeur's cap is pushed back on a ruddy expanse of forehead; a worn pair of sheepskin mittens lies on the table by his left hand. Allison, who loves to tell a story, one ice-blue eye fixed on his audience, telling of the things he has known and heard from others.

"But you know, Bill . . ." He is speaking to Melvin . . . "And Haines, here—we mustn't forget him, you know. There's been some pretty strange things happened up here in our day—fellas too long out there on the trapline by themselves, and some of them a little funny in the head to begin with, if you know what I mean."

And Melvin is nodding in agreement, a little wary of Allison's stories, but willing enough to listen. He him-

3

self has lived over forty years at Richardson, and at 78 is its oldest resident. His white hair is cropped above a strong, angular face, and upon his compact, wool-trousered frame he carries the alertness of a confident age. And he is saying in a quiet voice and with a level gaze directed to Allison that, yes, he knew of this or that person and event.

Then Allison, stirring his coffee with a heavy spoon, begins a story about two trappers who met and did not speak.

Solitary men in remote watersheds, each of them with a cabin and a team of dogs. And the winter wears on, the days briefer and darker, and then perceptibly a little longer and brighter. Circles are drawn around the calendar dates, and the leaves turned one by one. Silence, too much of it sometimes: the sound of frost cracking in the walls of the cabin, a wind in the spruce boughs overhead; the dogs barking at feeding time or howling at some distant wild voice. The same thoughts in the evenings, having come in from the cold and the long day out; the same pages read from the same catalogues and magazines; the same words muttered in some argument with the shadows. The same fat and cornmeal cooked in the big pot for the dogs at the same time each night; sleep, and the same light growing pale in the window late in the morning.

At last he must see someone, he feels. Not to talk, that would be too much; but just to see someone, to be with another person for a while. He knows of another trapper a long day's travel away on another creek. What is his name? It doesn't matter, he has to go. The sled is packed and the dogs harnessed. The morning is

4

mild, and off he goes, breaking a new trail through the snow to his distant neighbor.

It was already dusk when he drove in sight of a low-roofed, roughly-built cabin in spruce timber on a bench above a swampy creek. Someone was home, for smoke stood white and still above the short pipe in the snow roof. The dogs chained in the yard set up a din of barking at the strange team come so suddenly out of the trees.

He stopped his sled a little ways off at the edge of the woods with a grunted command to his dogs. As he unhitched and anchored his team for the night, the cabin door opened and another man stood framed in the doorway, looking at him across the cleared space of yard. He neither waved nor spoke, but turned back into the cabin, leaving the door ajar.

The man who had just arrived threw each of his dogs a chunk of frozen, half-dried fish from a bale on his sled. He took up his bedroll and walked through the yard, making his way among the five big dogs chained to their shelters, and who strained toward him, barking at his strangeness. When he reached the door of the cabin under the gable end of the roof he paused and looked back across the yard into the dusk. Then, stooping under the low doorframe, he stepped inside and closed the door behind him.

He found the other man seated on a bench at the single table in the light of a lantern just lit: a man much like himself, a little older, maybe, with a graying stubble on his face, and with a thoughtful and piercing gaze.

The man who had just come into the cabin set his

bedding on the floor. He took off his parka, shook it to remove the frost, and hung it from a spike near the door. He placed his mittens and his cap to dry on a rack above the dented, sheet-iron stove, and turned toward the table. He did these things slowly and deliberately, as if unsure of his welcome. But the man who lived there nodded at him and motioned with his hand toward a small wooden keg upturned at the other end of the table.

The man who came sat down. He did not look again at his companion. He studied his hands for a moment and rubbed them, easing the stiffness from his finger-joints. He glanced around at the interior of the small cabin, observing the familiarity of it, a place much like the one he had left that morning: a squared room built of peeled logs and with a smoke-darkened roof of poles; a window set in one wall, a space of rough plank floor between stove and table strewn with wood chips and stray fingers of straw.

The other man rose from his bench. He found two scarred enameled metal plates in a box on a shelf behind the stove, bent forks and spoons, and laid them out on the table. He returned to the stove where a black pot bubbled with meat and beans. And the two men sat and spooned out the steaming stew to their plates, and ate in silence.

The evening passes. The two men sit quietly, drinking tea. One of them dozes from fatigue and the warmth of the cabin, and wakes again with a start. The other rises now and then to put more wood on the fire, to clear the table and fill the kettle with water, after which he returns to his bench. The fire cracks, the lantern snores monotonously, and the evening wears on in silence.

After a time, the man on the bench rises, attends to the fire once more, and prepares for bed, just as he does each night at this time. The other man stands and unrolls his bedding on the floor in the space between stove and table. Each man unties his moccasins and hangs them from a nail in one of the roof beams. Long socks, heavy shirts and trousers are removed, the two men standing with their backs half-turned to each other, as if shy of the sudden company. Undressed to grey underwear, the two men lie down. The mantle in the lantern slowly flares to an amber glow, and the light goes out with a soft pop. Someone sighs deeply and turns in his bedding. A figure of darkness sits in the cabin, looking out at starlight on the snow.

There will be years of this life, he thinks; of the slow dawns and their light on the snow; years of this country, of its solitude and quiet. Or it will change, become crowded with sounds and new people, and he will not understand. He himself will grow old, grey and stiff, bent to the cordwood and the trap. But for as long as he can walk or stand he will stay with this life of snow, of fur, of solitude and dogs.

Now something rises into his consciousness, something of his past, of the place he came from. Faces without names appear and fade, and there are one or two with names. Questions are put to him from the darkness into which he is sinking: voices, but they have grown strange to him. There is something that he knows and cannot put into words. He could never say to them, the shadows whose forms now fill his darkening mind, why he came here, chose this life without company, without solace of children or ease for his age. He hardly remembers the reasons, the long ago decisions. There was the finality of leaving, of saying goodbye; a landscape he would not see again, a people he would never hear from. All that has become part of an immense distance, part of a sleeping self.

Morning came early, much earlier than the slow grey light at the single window. It came as a gradual chill to the cabin, as a muffled chain-rattle in the yard where a dog emerged from its shelter to stretch and shake itself.

The man sleeping on the bunk yawned and threw back his blankets. He sat up briefly in the dim light before striking a match and lighting the candle wedged in the end of an empty tin on a box beside the bunk. He rose to his feet in the yellow, flickering light and, avoiding with care the prone figure on the floor, with torn strips of birch bark and fine dry kindling he fired the stove, then filled the kettle with water from a bucket.

As the fire drew and crackled, the other man moved in his blankets and sat up. He saw the shadowy configuration of the room around him, was aware of the presence of another man, and knew he was not in his own place. As the small room warmed, he dressed himself and rolled up his bedding, while his silent companion moved with care between the stove and the table.

Soon there was coffee, oatmeal with raisins, and sourdough bread in a pan. And neither man said a word to the other, each one absorbed in his thoughts. From long habit, each of them knew the right thing to do at that hour: a glance out the door at the morning sky, another look with the candle at the thermometer on the wall outside the window. An armful of wood for the stove, a bucket of snow for water. And each returned to his bench or his keg, to sit once more looking into some deep shadow in the room.

It was full daylight now, as full as the brief winter day would allow: a rose-grey light beyond the hills to the south, a transparent twilight on the snow. It was time for him to leave.

The man who came tugged the laces of his moccasins and tied them. He stood up and took his mittens from the rack, his parka from the wall, his bedding from the floor. He paused, as if now finally he would speak, half-turned to the man still sitting beside the table. Then he opened the door and stepped out into the yard.

His moccasins made a dry, crunching sound on the packed snow as he walked to the edge of the woods where his dogs were standing, roused and shaking themselves, beginning to whine. He broke his sled loose from the snow and packed it once more. His movements were quick and sure now. He laid the cold, stiff harness out on the snow, and one by one he snapped his dogs into the towline.

The other man came to the door of the cabin. He stood watching as the man at the edge of the yard spoke something quietly to his dogs, and they moved off swiftly onto the broken trail, heading home.

Allison pours a little rum into his cup and shoves the bottle across the table. I see the familiar red and yellow label: *Lemon Hart, Demarara Rum, 151 Proof.* Melvin is watching in his guarded and knowing way; he will have no more rum, at his age he doesn't drink much. I cannot tell if he believes the story, but he smiles a little crookedly and looks at me from under shaggy eyebrows as if he would share with me some comment that he cannot speak aloud.

I have said little, sitting across the table from Allison. I am silent because I am young, and because I have almost nothing to tell; it is my place to listen now, watching the faces and gestures of these two men long past their youth.

The talk goes on: questions, assertions, a careful sparring among things remembered, called up on impulse from years shared in a country whose thinly-settled people have been like members of a restless family. And as I listen, something fills the pauses and surges in their talk, as in some interval of quiet comes now and then a sigh from the great range by the kitchen wall. I find myself for a time included in a vanished company—of men camped or on the move, hunting, tree-falling, digging, sometimes together and often apart. Their voices rise and fade: guttural exclamations, curses and impatient whispers. From Kansas, Ontario, Michigan—yoked to the single, confused prospect . . . . With chain and whip, by wagon and sledge, by boat and rail, and by foot; over soaked sod and dry snow, drawn forward with creaking axles and squealing runners. They pass, knotted and dispersed, in a solitude without women.

Who comes here, to this whiteness, this far and frozen place, in search of something he cannot name? Not wealth, it may be, but a fortune of the spirit, a freshness denied him in the place he came from. The North glitters and brightens; the land grows dark again, and the fugitive glow from a gas mantle lights the shadows.

Allison fills the cups with coffee, pouring out of a big blue granite pot brought from the stove. He stands beside the table in a half-buttoned, dark brown sweater—a short man in his late sixties, erect and broad in the chest. Now he takes the lantern down from its hook in the ceiling. He closes a thumb over the end of the pump rod and works it. The mantles brighten, and the sound of the forced and burning air grows loud again.

Now Melvin remembers something about a bear. I imagine he knows as much about bears and about the woods as any man I have met; certainly he has forgotten more than I will ever know. And quietly, as of something chosen at ease from a great storehouse, he begins to tell how once, long years ago, he traveled through the Stewart River country with a party of men on foot.

It was getting on toward the middle of fall, and they were on their way back to Dawson from a recent stampede, eager to record their staked parcels of ground and return to the creeks before winter caught them. Late one afternoon they caught up with a big grizzly who was walking the trail before them. With the bear in sight ahead, the party halted.

They were in a narrow canyon of the river, on a trail recently cleared by a telegraph crew. The river lay sheerly below them on one side, and a steep rock face pitched above them on the other. There was no way around that bear, and strangely in that party of stampeders, no one had brought a gun.

11

The bear himself was in no hurry, rolling fat and densely-haired, heading into winter. The hump on his black shoulders rippled as he moved along. Becoming aware of the men behind him, he turned and rose to his full height, peering toward them where they were gathered in a group sixty yards away. Then, satisfied they were no threat to him, the bear dropped back to all fours and went leisurely on his way.

The men camped at nightfall as well as they could on the narrow shelf of the trail, making a scanty fire from the few dry sticks and tough green shrubs they found on the slopes around them. They hoped the bear would be gone next day. Winter was coming, a little snow in the air at times; food was low, and none of them knew the country well; they were anxious to be in town.

But soon after breaking camp in the morning, as they picked their way on the rough trail with their heavy packs, they caught up with the bear again. And there they waited. It was his country and his season, and he was not going to be pushed. Impatient, but with no other choice, they traveled the day at the bear's deliberate pace.

For three days the party was forced to walk behind that bear. It was a slow and exasperating journey, the bear taking time to dig for roots along the trail, upending rocks in search of mice. Or he would stop at any time of the day to sleep, sprawled out in the middle of the trail like a great rugheap, stretching his long-nailed, hairy toes and snapping his jaws in the air, while the men watched from a distance.

One or two of the men, more foolish than the rest, got angry. They shouted at the bear and threw rocks toward him. Unused to any animals but dogs and horses, the bear to them was only a big nuisance, an unruly pet, a zoo creature out of place in the landscape. They were lucky in their ignorance, for the bear only turned and growled at them if they came too close.

Then, late in the third day, as they approached a wooded break in the canyon, the bear, who was now only a short distance ahead of them, stopped again. He turned, rose once more to a thick and imposing presence, and looked steadily at the men gathered behind him. They could see plainly the thick dark fur of him, slightly ruffled by a breeze, shining in the thin fall sunlight that came from across the river through a gap in the canyon wall. The big, round face of the bear regarded them, his blunt nose searching the air. It was the assured and measuring look of the undisputed master of things.

Finally and, as it seemed, with great dignity, the bear dropped down again and turned away. As if he had known all along exactly where he was going, he climbed easily among some tumbled boulders, and with a muffled cracking of dry brush he vanished uphill in the scattered timber.

Melvin is quiet again. He has none of Allison's flair for drama, but speaks matter-of-factly, and never insists on an audience. Another time, when he and I are alone in his cabin by the river, he will talk, the far away things he remembers coming almost casually if he thinks I want to hear.

We drink, coffee or rum, and a few more words are spoken on the subject of bears. There are names and incidents: Fred Campbell, for instance, and his loose-running pack of dogs, chasing every bear in the country to keep the dogs fed. A damned nuisance, Melvin says; no one could find a moose because of the commotion he raised.

I learn of bears in the Democrat cookhouse, rattling the pots and dishes, pulling down shelves and boxes, while the men listening from the next room through the log wall plotted how to chase them out. Of a bear named Teddie that Melvin raised from a cub, keeping him tamed with a stout stick, until in its fourth year the bear became surly and aggressive and had to be shot.

A chronicle of the wise, the foolish and the lucky—it will be resumed one evening when we are here again, to renew the playful innocence of an early day when men could stand in wonder at a beast, to marvel at a world abundant with things that walked and flew and swam and seemed possessed of understanding, to speak at times almost like men themselves.

From somewhere back in my own memory now I pull together a few phrases from a far more recent spring. They tell in the plain prose of a daily newspaper how a well-known big-game guide and his wealthy hunter, missing for over a week in the Alaska Range, had been found dead, killed by the grizzly they had tried to smoke from his den. It was front page Interior news at the time, one of those stories that stamp the season with the unmistakable aura of tragedy or adventure. And I remember so well how old Delmar Elliot, a long-gone neighbor, talked about it as we drove along one morning on the road into Fairbanks. He related the story as he had heard it, from start to finish, methodically, in detail, as if he wanted the story told right for some page of local history, and concluding in his flat-toned, serious way: "The bear bit 'em . . . I guess that's why they died."

But it is deep winter now, and all the bears are sleeping. There are other things to think of—keeping warm, for instance. Allison, turning the bottle of rum in a broad hand, mentions a name: Jim Chisholm, who owned a cabin on Birch Lake back in the 'thirties. A drinking man, single, past middle age, careless with stove and fire.

And one cold night in December, when he had stoked the fire too hot and gone to bed, sparks from a bad pipe-joint caught in the dry roof-moss above the stove. Chisholm was roused from heavy sleep by the heat and smoke of a fire burning at one end of the cabin—hot flames eating the dry poles as if they were paper. Confused, clad only in a thin nightshirt, he had time and thought to grab a robe and thrust his feet into a pair of slippers before he ran through the blazing doorway to the snow outside.

It was thirty below and thinly overcast, one of those nights when you must look a long time to see the far shore of a lake. Chisholm stood in the glarelit darkness in slippers and loose robe, half-warmed by his blazing cabin, as log after log caught, and then a part of the roof came down in a shower of sparks.

Two miles distant across the snow and ice of the lake were his nearest neighbors in a lodge on the Valdez road. With nothing left to him in the fire and settling ashes, he turned toward the icebound lake and began to walk.

It was a long walk in daylight on a firm trail. Chisholm plowed along, missing the trail, stumbling in the dry, lightly-drifted snow that came at times to his knees. He was urged on by a growing fear, as he held his arms crossed on his chest, clutching the robe to his body, its narrow collar partly wrapped about his face and ears. He no longer felt the cold snow in his slippers, but sensed instead a pricking numbness growing upward into his legs. He was fully awake and breathing hard, staring into the snow, into the wind that came now and then across the frozen lake, toward what he thought he could see half-lighted in the timber on the far shore.

In the kitchen of the small roadhouse at the south end of the lake, two men whose names are not recorded were drinking late coffee and washing up for the night. There was little traffic in the winter, sixty miles out from Fairbanks, and at that late hour no travelers were expected. But afterwhile in the stillness they heard a sound outside, a slow and measured thumping on the steps that rose to the porch.

Here, Allison, in a dramatic gesture, lifted the bottle of rum and brought it down on the table . . . bump . . . bump . . . bump . . . That was the sound they heard.

One of the men went to the door with a lantern and opened it to the night. And there in the still cold was Chisholm, coming slowly across the snow-cleared boards. His robe clung loosely about him, he had long since lost his slippers. He lifted each leg as if it was made of wood, and let the bare, hard foot fall with a heavy thump. And then he stopped and stood in the light of the lantern, peering out from the frost that clung to his hair and the collar of his robe, unable to lift

16

his head or unclasp his arms, unable to speak for the great cold that was in him.

The two men, roused into action, brought him into the warmth of the kitchen and sat him down in a chair before the stove. They did it gently, with care not to bruise or break his frozen flesh. A blanket was warmed and wrapped about him. Hot coffee was poured and brought to him, the cup tilted to his lips, a little at a time, until he could speak and could tell what had happened.

His feet and lower legs were like dead things, nearly hard and white as marble. It looked bad, but something had to be done. A five gallon tin of coal oil was standing in the kitchen, warm from the heat of the room. A washtub was brought in from the pantry and set on the floor by the stove. Chisholm's feet were placed within it, and the coal oil was carefully poured into the tub. One man knelt on the floor by the tub and began to massage his legs with the warm oil, lifting it with his hands, rubbing down from the stiff knees, letting the skin and numbed flesh soften as he worked.

An hour passed, and something more than an hour, as the men traded places on the floor beside the tub. As they worked, and the surrounding warmth took effect, color gradually came back to Chisholm's face and body; very slowly sensation returned to his legs and feet, and with it a terrible pain.

"Well, you know," said Allison, leaning toward us and gripping the rum bottle in his hand, "it took both of those fellas to hold him down in the chair when the feeling came back in his feet. He yelled and moaned and fought like hell, but they saved him. I tell you, old

Chisholm was pretty damned lucky. He may have lost a couple of toes, but he walked on those feet and legs till the day he died."

The bottle of rum stands on the table before us, the dark liquor a few fingers down in the brown glass. Allison stares at us across the gleaming oilcloth with his one good eye, having spoken with a kind of finality, the slim note of affirmation still on his lips. So ends that story, as true as any you'll hear.

It is late, nearly midnight. Allison yawns and pushes his chair back from the table. He must bring in another bucket of coal and check the fire for the night. Melvin agrees it is time for him to be going. Time too for me to walk that mile and a half uphill to home.

We all get to our feet and reach for our mitts and parkas. Allison follows us out to the door, carrying the lantern and an empty scuttle.

Through the opened door a sudden rush of cold air comes in from the night. We stand a moment together on the porch to see the stars. Clear frost tonight, maybe ten below—not so bad. "Pretty good winter so far, by golly!"

"Goodnight, Bill. Goodnight, Haines. See you soon." Allison's words are followed by the sound of a shovel grating on the frozen, gravelly earth. A bulky figure bending in the lantern light by the coalshed, the nodding, deliberate movements of his arms and body are lengthened into shadows on the snow.

Melvin says goodnight in a clear voice; he walks across the road, a flashlight held before him, walking firmly toward his cabin, a quarter mile off by the river.

I begin walking the road in the other direction,

toward Banner Creek, into the snow-lighted darkness. Under starlight, the snow glitters faintly. The shadowy, wooded crest of Richardson Hill rises before me. My moccasins crunch softly in the roadside snow. There is no other sound in the night. Nothing, not even the wind.

# Out of the Shadows

IT WAS EARLY in July. I was on my way to Cabin Creek, eight miles distant by trail in the Redmond drainage. I intended to make a quick overnight trip to secure our hunting cabin for the season and to see what the prospects might be for blueberries later that summer.

For company I had brought with me our youngest dog, a female husky named Moppet. She was nearly two years old, a quiet, alert and intelligent animal. Glad to be along, to have been chosen, she trotted ahead of me on the trail, the thick grey and white plume of her tail swinging from side to side.

I was carrying my big pack basket containing a small ax, some food, and an old sweater to wear in the evening. I was also carrying one of the two rifles I owned, an ancient 8mm Mannlicher carbine I had inherited from an old resident in the country. It had once been a fighting weapon of the German Army in World War I. It had a scarred stock and a worn barrel, but was compact and light and easy to carry.

We had left home early to take advantage of the morning coolness. Now, five miles out, with the sun high at our backs on the open, sloping bench above Redmond Creek, the mid-morning was clear and warm. As always here, the trail was wet underfoot, the moss and the dark sod still soaking from the spring runoff. Mosquitoes and small gnats rose out of the moss; a continual and shifting cloud of them swarmed about us.

As we walked along, skirting one dark pool of meltwater after another, I was thinking of many things: of the summer before me, of the fishing about to begin, the hoped-for success of the summer garden, and not too far ahead another hunting season. I took casual note of the places where in the winter just past I had set my traps: a shelter of twigs and sticks fallen together, and every so often under the lower boughs of a spruce tree standing near the trail a rusty marten trap was hanging, wired to its toggle stick.

It was a typical summer day in the subarctic backcountry. I was alone with a dog in a country that with its creeks, ridges and divides, and with the high, brown slope of Banner Dome visible to the north, was as familiar to me as any suburban backyard. On the changing features of the landscape I seemed to see written my own signature of use.

We rounded the steep spruce-clad prow of the hill above Glacier Creek and stopped briefly at a cache I kept there below the point of hill. Here, three years before and late in the fall, we had camped in a tent while hunting moose. The ground poles of our tent were lying where we had left them under the trees. It was not hard for me to visualize things as they had been then: the grey slope of the canvas tent, smoke from the stovepipe and snow in the wind. For a few weeks that tent had been home. Moppet was not yet born. Now I looked up at the narrow platform of the cache fixed solidly in the three spruces above me. A half dozen traps were hanging from a spike in one of the supports. The ridge pole of the tent and the rest of its framework were pitched together and standing upright against the cache to keep them dry. I saw that everything was as I had left it when I stopped here with the dogs and sled on the last snow of the season.

We left the cache and went on down the trail toward the creek. The brush was thick, of dense, small-statured black spruce interspersed with thickets of alders. The trail wound about so that at no time could I see more than thirty feet ahead of me. Moppet was now out of sight somewhere ahead and probably waiting for me at the crossing.

As I came out of the woods and onto the open bench above the creek, I saw Moppet sitting at the edge of the steep slide down which the trail led to the creek bottom. Her ears were pricked sharply forward, and she was staring intently at something in the creek.

When I came up to her, I saw what she was watching. Down in the creek and less than twenty yards away, the shoulders and back of a large brown creature showed above the heavy summer grass and clumps of ice-cropped willows. It was moving slowly downstream at the far edge of an island that divided the creek.

At first I thought the animal was a young moose feeding on the fresh grass or on some waterplants in the shallow streamcourse. And yet there was something about its size and bulk and the way that it was moving that was not quite familiar. And then the creature's head came into partial view, and I saw how the brown hump of its shoulders rippled as it moved. It was a bear, larger than any bear I had yet seen in that country. One look at that heavy square head and the shoulder hump, and I knew we had met a grizzly.

No more than a minute passed as I stood there with

Moppet at my feet, watching the big bear in the grass below us. I was glad now that I had not brought one of our other dogs who would have immediately rushed barking into the creek after the bear. I was grateful for this quiet and obedient animal sitting at my feet with her hair stiffened on her shoulders and her nose twitching.

Where I stood at that moment I had an easy shot broadside into the bear's chest or shoulders. I could perhaps have killed it then and there. But I did not want to leave a dead bear to rot in the creek, and we were too far from home to pack out more than a small portion of the meat.

In the brief time that we stood there, I quickly went over my choices. We could not proceed down into the creek and follow the trail across to the opposite bank; the bear was by now directly in our path. We could stay where we were and let the bear go on downstream if that was its intention. But would Moppet remain quiet long enough?

I thought of easing away from the scene, of moving upstream far enough to cross without disturbing the bear. It would have to be done quickly and quietly. At any moment the bear might discover us, or the noise of our retreat might alarm it. In an emergency there were no trees large enough to climb, and there was no hope of outrunning an aroused bear in that wet and spongy ground. My one advantage lay in the fact that we were above the bear and that it had not yet discovered us.

But the bear soon left me no choice. Something in our unseen presence on the bank above the creek, some sound, some prickling sense that it was not alone, seemed to change the bear's intentions. It stopped feeding. Its head came up, and it began to move more rapidly through the grass. As it did so, it turned in our direction. It was now in full view, no more than fifty feet away, and closing the distance between us.

In my sudden alarm that grizzly loomed larger and more of a threat than any black bear or bull moose I had ever met with. I was ready to fire, but in those swift moments I thought I might be able to frighten the bear, and by some noise or movement scare it back into the woods. Still holding my rifle, I raised my arms over my head. In what seems now to have been a ridiculous gesture, I waved my arms and did a small dance on the moss; I yelled and hooted and hoped. But the sudden noise, coming out of the stillness, seemed only to panic the animal. It broke into a loping run, heading directly toward us, and had already reached the bottom of the bank below us. I had no choice now. I put the rifle to my shoulder, took hurried aim at the heavy chest of hair below that big head, and fired.

At the sound of the gunshot the bear abruptly stopped a few feet below. It rose on its hind legs and stood at full height in front of us. In a rush of images I saw the stocky, upright length of its body, a patch of pale fur on its underthroat, the forepaws raised in a defensive gesture; I saw the blunt muzzle and the suddenly opened jaws. The bear growled loudly, swung its head to one side, and tried to bite at its chest. I was ready to fire again, and at that moment I might have put a shot squarely into its thick neck or broad upper chest. But for some reason in those tense seconds I again held my fire.

The bear dropped back to the ground. It turned away from us and ran back through the grass and brush in a tremendous, lunging gallop, scattering leaves and splashing water. I watched it climb the bank on the opposite side of the creek and disappear. A heavy crashing came from the dry alders on the far side, and then all was still.

I stood at the top of the bank with my rifle half-raised, listening. Over everything in that sudden stillness I was aware of my heart as a loud pounding above the calm trickle of water in the creek below. I heard a low whine, and glanced down. All this time Moppet had remained crouched and quiet at my feet. But now she rose with her fur bristling, searching the air with her nose, trying to catch some scent of that enormous creature so suddenly discovered and now vanished.

I moved away from the trail and walked a short distance upstream to where a bulky, crooked spruce grew at the edge of the bank. It was as large as any tree in the vicinity, and for some reason I felt more comfortable standing close to it. I removed my pack and set it on the ground beside me. I placed my rifle against the tree while I searched in my shirt pocket for tobacco and papers. In those days I was an occasional smoker. With trembling hands I rolled a cigarette, lit it, and smoked in silence.

It had all happened so quickly. Perhaps no more than three minutes had elapsed since I had first seen the bear. Now that I had some space in which to think, I realized that I had been extremely lucky. Had the bear not stopped, a second shot might have killed it, but if not there would have been no way I could have escaped at least a severe mauling.

Somehow in that blur of excitement and indecision, I knew that I would not turn and run. Out of whatever stubborn sense of my own right to be there, or simply from an obscure pride, I would stand my ground, fire my shot, and from then on fend off the wounded bear as best I could, using my rifle for a club. In that event I would most likely have been killed, or I would have been so badly maimed that I could never have made it home without help, and there was no help anywhere near. Days might have passed before anyone came looking for me.

I stood there and smoked, gradually coming to some calm in myself. I could hear nothing from the woods on the far side of the creek. There was not the slightest movement to be seen in the brush growing upon that low bank, nothing at all in the grass below. From time to time I gazed up or down the creek as far as I could see above the willows and alders. Nothing.

I did not know how badly hit that bear was. Perhaps it was now lying dead over there. Or it might only be wounded, lying in the brush near the trail, gathering its strength and waiting for me to pass. At such times events and probabilities seem magnified; fear has a thousand faces.

I finished my cigarette, and picked up my pack and my rifle. I knew that I would have to go down into the creek and search the sand and grass for blood. Whatever I found, I would follow the bear's path across the creek and into the woods. I wanted above all to be on my way to the cabin and out of any further trouble. But first I had to be sure of that bear.

I waited another few minutes. Then, with Moppet at my heels, I returned to the trail, and we began our descent into the creek.

At the bottom of the bank I easily found the place

27

where the bear had stood up after I fired at him. His big tracks were pressed deeply into the wet sand, the long toenails and the pad marks clearly outlined at the edge of the small channel.

Slowly and quietly I began to trace the bear's path through the grass. Stopping frequently to look around me over the grass and through the brush, I followed as well as I could the paw marks in the sand and the muddy sod. Where I could not see his tracks, I guided myself by the bent and broken grasses in the deep trough of the bear's passage. As I walked, half-crouched, searching the ground, I examined with care every blade of grass and every leaf on the willows. But I found no sign of blood.

We went on through the grass and brush. Across the far channel we found the trail, climbed the shallow bank and entered the woods. Moppet remained at my heels, at times pressing closely against my leg. Though I tried quietly to coax her, she would not go ahead but stayed close behind. The fur on her shoulders and neck was stiffened, and as she looked from side to side into the woods a muted and anxious throaty sound came from her, half growl and half whine.

Once up the bank and into the woods, we stopped. It was spooky as hell under that shadowy, sun-broken canopy of leaves. I searched the woods around me for the slightest movement and listened for any sound: a wounded breathing, a growl, anything. Nowhere in all that wilderness could I hear a sound above the muted purling of water in the creek behind me, and the song of a fox sparrow somewhere in the watercourse.

We walked on, following the trail where it skirted the edge of a narrow ravine holding a wayward tributary of the creek. To cross the ravine I had built a rough bridge out of spruce poles. On the far side the trail turned upstream and continued through a swamp toward Cabin Creek.

When Moppet and I had crossed the bridge, I stopped again. Here an old game trail, deeply-cut into the moss, intersected our sled trail and took its narrow, twisting way downstream. I hesitated. Nothing I had seen so far convinced me that the bear was at all wounded, but I was still not satisfied. I stepped into the game trail and began a careful circuit of the downstream woods into which I had seen the bear vanish. As quiet as it was, as eerily still, I felt that somewhere in that dim tangle of alders, willows and dwarf birch the bear must be lying and listening to our movements. As in an episode of warfare, a pervasive uneasiness seemed to divide the shadows and the sunlight. I had that acute sense of being watched and listened to by an invisible foe. Each twig-snap and wave of a bough seemed a potential signal.

After about twenty minutes of what I considered to be a reasonably careful search, I returned to the trail. I now felt, from the lack of any bloodsign or other evidence, that the bear had not been badly hit. I decided not to pursue the search any further. With Moppet following me, I went on through the swamp, climbing steadily toward the saddle that divided Glacier from Cabin Creek. We went carefully, every so often stopping to look back down the trail behind us. We were well away from the creek before Moppet would put aside her fear and go ahead of me.

It seemed to me now that I had merely grazed the underside of the bear's chest. I had fired downhill at a running target, and had aimed low. Moreover, the front sight of the old carbine had been damaged years ago and repaired with solder in a makeshift fashion. The gunsight was uncertain at best.

So obviously I had fired too low, and the bear had suffered no more than a nasty sting from the heavy 230 grain bullet I was using. Had the bear been solidly hit, there would surely have been blood somewhere, and there would by now be a dead or dying bear in the woods. As we came down off the hill on the last half mile stretch to the cabin I began to feel a great deal easier, satisfied that I had not left a badly wounded animal behind me, and glad too that we had gotten off from the encounter ourselves with no more trouble.

We spent the night at the cabin. I fed Moppet and cut some firewood. In the late afternoon I did a few needed chores about the cabin. On going to the creek for a bucket of water, I found a few unripe blueberries among the bushes overhanging the deep, wet moss hummocks beside the creek. The berries were scattered, and it did not seem to me that they would be worth a trip later to pick them. As the evening light deepened over the hills and the air grew cooler, a thrush sent up its spiraling song from the aspens on the hillside across the creek. Mosquitoes whined at the screen door. Otherwise, things were very quiet there on the hill above Cabin Creek.

The following morning I secured the cabin for the remainder of the summer. I set a strong barricade over the door, and closed and nailed heavy shutters over the two windows. In the late morning Moppet and I set out for home.

As we came down through the swamp near Glacier, Moppet once more dropped behind me and refused to go ahead. I walked quietly with the rifle safety off and my hand half-closed on the trigger. Again I watched the brush and listened to either side of the trail for the slighest sound. There was nothing but the quiet sunlit air of a summer day.

We crossed the creek, striding the small channels and pushing aside the grass, and on the far side we climbed the bank again. When we came to the top, I looked down. There, squarely in the trail and almost exactly where I had stood the day before when I fired at the bear, was a fresh mound of bear dropping. Nearby lay the spent shell from my rifle.

I looked closely at the dropping. It contained a few unripe blueberries, seeds and other matter. It was still wet, though not warm. Moppet sniffed at it, and the grizzled hair once more rose on her neck and shoulders. For a moment my uneasiness returned, that vague, shivery sense of being watched and followed. The bear was still around, alive and well. Dangerous? I had no way of knowing.

The bear had probably not run far on the previous day, but had found a place in which to lie and lick its wound, baffled as to the source of its sudden hurt. It had heard us pass on the trail, had heard every sound of my passage in the brush, had followed every detail of my search. Perhaps much later in the evening it came out of its hiding place, out of the late cool shadows, and returned to the trail. It had stood where we were standing now, with its great, shaggy head down, sniffing the moss, the wet, black sod, trying to place in its dim sense of things an identity it would carry with it for the rest of its life.

I looked back down into the grass and brush of the creek from which we had just come. I turned and looked ahead of me to where the stubby black spruce wood closed in around the trail. If the bear was still somewhere in that dense green cover, nursing its hurt and its temper, waiting for revenge, it would have its chance.

But nothing vengeful and bloody came out of the woods to meet us as we went on up the trail. The walk home by Redmond, the long uphill climb to the homestead ridge passed without further incident. We came down off the hill as on many another occasion, to the sunlit vista of the river and the highway, to the sound of the dogs' furious barking. I had a good story to tell, and Moppet was petted and praised for her wise behavior.

In many subsequent hikes over the trail to Cabin Creek, in hunting forays along the benches above Glacier, we never saw that bear again. Now and then in late summer and early fall a blue mound of dropping in the trail gave evidence of a bear in the country, and that was all.

Never before or since have I been so rattled on meeting an animal in the woods. Years later, when I began to think of writing these pages, I rehearsed for myself another outcome to the adventure. I described in detail how the bear, badly hit in its lungs, had waited in the brush on the far side of the creek. When Moppet and I went by on the trail, the bear suddenly lunged from its hiding place with a terrible, bubbling roar and struck me down.

In that instant of confusion and shock I was joined to the hot blood and rank fur at last. All my boyhood dreams of life in the woods, of courage and adventure, had come to this final and terrifying intimacy.

Following the initial shock, as I lay sprawled by the trail with the bear standing hot and wounded above me, I managed to regain a grip on my rifle. Though stunned and, as it seemed, half blinded, I raised the short muzzle of that ancient weapon and got off one last shot into the bear's throat. And with the sound of that shot in my ears, I lost consciousness.

In what may have been an hour or only minutes, I returned to a dazed sense of myself. I sat up, struggling to free myself of the things that seemed to hold me: my pack harness, torn clothing, and bits of broken brush. I seemed to look at myself and my surroundings from a great distance through a sun-dazzled semi-darkness. I was still alive, though in the numbed, head-ringing silence I knew I was hurt, badly cut and bitten about my face and body. Moppet was gone. A short distance away from me the bear lay dead.

Somehow, maimed, stiffened and bleeding, using a dry stick for a crutch, I found my way home. Patched and scarred, I wore my changed face as an emblem of combat, and walked in my damaged body to the end of my days, survivor of a meeting terrible and true.

# Burning a Porcupine

I HAVE NEVER eaten a porcupine. The seasonal abundance of meat, fish, berries and garden food made the taking of such animals unnecessary. But the dogs had to be fed by whatever means; between fish runs the pot was sometimes lean, and a small amount of fat meat went a long way.

In those rich Interior summers, when so many creature-things were awake, breeding and flourishing, it was not difficult to find a porcupine. Sometimes one would show up in the yard or the garden in the evening, shuffling through on its blind, mysterious travel. Often it was the dogs, turned loose for a run, who would find it. We heard a furious barking up the creek, and soon enough a dog came home with a dose of quills in its nose. Backtracking the woods, I found the mild, offending creature still holding its ground. A sharp blow on its blunt, black snout was sufficient to kill it: the stout, quill-bristled body slowly relaxing, a light in the dull, black eyes growing dim.

With the porcupine dead, came the preparation and use of the meat. The quills, those fiery-pointed arrows so lethal to dogs and other predators, had to be gotten rid of. There was a method, as there always is, a right way to do a thing. Years ago I learned how to burn a porcupine from Fred Campbell one late summer day at his lake camp, far in the headwater hills behind Richardson.

We had caught the porky on our way back from

McCoy Creek the previous evening. We heard Fred's dogs barking somewhere ahead of us on the trail, and knew they had found either a bear or a porcupine. Listening, I could not have said which it was, but Fred, from the shrill intensity of the din, guessed that it was a porky and that the dogs had it cornered.

There is the rare dog that in a given instance seems to know what needs to be done; when a porcupine is found the dog will stand back away from the quills, seeming to know that the creature is going to be killed, and that the killing means meat. Campbell had such a dog, an ugly, scarred bitch named Judy, who with a sure sense of purpose always managed to corner the porky and keep it until he arrived.

We found the porcupine making a stand with its head lowered and its rear end armed with that powerful, quill-studded tail exposed to the excited dogs. One of the younger dogs had a few quills in its nose; wise Judy, standing well back and out of reach, barked and waited.

Fred killed the porcupine with his walking stick, a good solid blow on its head. He flipped it over and gutted it on the spot, dividing the liver with his knife and tossing a piece of it to each of his dogs. He placed the entrails high in a tree-crotch out of reach—the intestines were likely to be full of worms, and it was best not to let the dogs have any part of them raw.

We pulled the few quills from the one dog's nose, and packed up. Even with the guts removed, the dead weight of the porcupine made a heavy load in Fred's pack basket. We had had a long day, but we were close to camp and the meat was needed.

The following day Fred took the cooled body of the

porcupine down from the roof of his cabin where he had cached it during the night. I was curious as to how he was going to remove the quills in order to feed the meat to the dogs. I ventured the observation that it would be a damned nuisance to skin it. Fred only grunted and told me to watch if I wanted to learn.

In the grassy yard in front of the cabin he scraped away a patch of sod to expose the sandy mineral soil underneath. He gathered up some dry sticks of wood, and with a strip of birch bark he built a small fire. As soon as the flames were leaping out of the brushwood, he placed the carcass of the porcupine on the fire. Immediately a plume of white and yellow smoke rose, and with it the sour, pungent smell of burning hair.

Fred adjusted the carcass on the fire, lifting it now and then to prevent it from smothering the flames. As the quills were singed, he took a short stick and beat the burned section clean, then turned the porky on the fire to expose another patch of hair and quills to the flames. Where the heat was intense, fat bubbled from the hide and dripped on the flames that flared up in a sudden, intenser blaze.

Those of Fred's dogs that were loose paced around the shifting smoke-haze, waiting for a burned piece of meat to come their way; the others, chained to their houses, followed every detail with eyes that seemed to blaze up with every flare of the fire.

And so it went, the fire replenished if need be, the carcass turned and returned. The singeing and the beating with a stick continued until all the hair and quills were burned off, and the scorched and blackened body was bare.

With the quills gone, Fred laid the carcass on a wood

block, and with a sharp axe he chopped choice pieces of the meat and bone into the five gallon tin bucket that served as a dogpot. He returned what was left of the porcupine to the cabin roof, out of reach of the dogs.

Later that evening he cooked the meat and bones, thickening the broth with cornmeal to make a stout, rich porridge. When done, the brew was set aside to cool for the night; it was fed to the dogs next day.

In the years that followed that afternoon, living the woods life in all its varied fullness, I burned my score of porcupines. I built my fire of sticks in the yard and singed the quills, beating them off with a stick in the way I had learned, while my own dogs sat by and watched.

The thick, muscular tail of the porcupine particularly was a great source of fat meat, and a full-grown carcass would last for several days. While it was cooking, the meat smelled strong, a mingling of burned hair and fire-scorched hide. But afterwhile that smell became almost pleasant, concentrated and potent as it rose from the steaming pot in which the cornmeal bubbled with meat and fat.

Barbaric if you say so, but religious too in a strangely appropriate way, the quill-burning was one of the rites by which we lived and kept the seasons. I look back on it as an occasional sacrifice before the memory of a long-ago woods-spirit, the details of which were spare and essential: the brush fire kindled, the acrid white and yellow smoke spilling upward from the burned quills, the big pot sitting by, and the clean axe waiting. The smell of singed porcupine, the heavy, rich odor of the simmering broth lingered about the house and yard for days.

# Shadows

ONE AUGUST NIGHT, on the trail back from McCoy
Creek, Fred Campbell and I stopped to rest. The fall
darkness was coming on, and we had been walking for
the past hour in a very dim twilight. As we stood for a
moment, hunched under our packs and leaning on our
walking sticks, we heard overhead in the windless quiet
of the evening a small explosive sound, a snap or a
chirp, like nothing I had heard before.

"What was that?" I asked.

"Flying squirrel, I think."

Maybe once or twice afterwards in my night jour-
neys home through the woods I heard a sound like
that—a dry, sharp chirp in the trees above me, though I
could see nothing near me in the darkness. It was a
sound related to the creaking of tree limbs rubbed
together in the wind, a sound that belonged to the
night.

But late one winter a flying squirrel came to the bird
feeder set on a shelf by the house. It may have been
attracted by the window light, or had at dusk observed
the birds coming and going. Once it had discovered the
feeder, the squirrel came at dusk or after dark, seldom
by day, to feed on the cornmeal, bread scraps, suet and
seed put out for the winter chickadees and wood-
peckers.

We always knew when the squirrel arrived by the
sudden "thump" of its landing on the feeder roof. By
light of the one lamp set indoors by the window, we

watched it hunched in the cold, nibbling and alert: a compact, delicately formed creature, its rich fur grizzled grey and brown, a pale underbelly, and with the large dark eyes of a nocturnal animal. It soon became familiar enough to allow one of us to approach the feeder closely and put out more food. The squirrel barely paused in its munching of seeds, its dark eyes shining in the subdued glare of a flashlight.

One evening, just after sunset, when the flying squirrel had been at the house for a short time, I watched it leave the feeder. It sprang to the trunk of the large aspen that grew beside the house, climbed quickly to the top, and launched itself into the air toward a nearby birch. I saw it sail without difficulty to a landing on the lower trunk of the birch; it rapidly climbed that tree, from which it again launched itself into the forest.

Thinking later on that skilled and effortless flight in the dusk, I recalled how once years before I had in fun shaken a red squirrel from a tree to amuse the dogs. The squirrel was high in a slender willow, and there were no other trees of size close enough for it to jump to. As my shaking increased and the willow swayed back and forth, the squirrel, braced in the topmost branches, suddenly launched into the air. I saw it come down in a kind of slow-motion descent, its four legs outspread and tail held stiff and straight with the long hairs flattened; it seemed to float to the ground. It fell with a soft thump on the dry autumn sod not far from where I stood, having fallen a distance of more than thirty feet. It lay still for a moment; then, recovered from the shock of its landing, and before the dogs could grab it, it ran to the trunk of a larger tree nearby and climbed to safety.

In that brief exhibition of daring and skill I saw how a night-feeding squirrel might, given sufficient time, say a million years or so, stretch the loose skin of its body and develop that sailing skill to perfection.

Later in the spring a second flying squirrel came to the feeder, and there were two of them. They remained through the spring and well into the summer, and it began to look as if we might have them as permanent residents on the homestead. But one day we returned from a camping trip to find one of the squirrels floating face down in a rain barrel. The barrel stood near the southwest corner of the house, a few feet from the bird feeder; at the time the barrel was somewhat more than half-filled with water. Somehow the squirrel had fallen in and had been unable to climb out. Afterwards I put a screen over the barrel, but it was too late. The remaining squirrel never returned to the feeder.

And then the following winter a flying squirrel was found dead at the roadhouse. A door to one of the sheds had been left open, and the squirrel had apparently been attracted to a sack of dog food that was stored there. The door was then closed, and the squirrel, unable to get out, had frozen. It was curled up on a shelf in a hard little ball, a furry knot of frozen energy.

Knowing that I was an occasional trapper, the owner of the roadhouse asked me to skin the squirrel for him so that he could hang it on the wall of his bar as part of his fur collection.

I took the small, stiff animal home, so small that it fitted easily into the pocket of my parka. I thawed it out and carefully skinned it. After some trial, I fashioned a thin, flat board on which to stretch the delicate pelt. It stretched out more or less square, about seven by eight inches, its thin flying membrane of skin and hair attached like a cape or a sail between the tiny, clawed forefeet and hind feet. The dry pelt with its soft, rich fur made a pleasing pattern of contrasting brown and cream color edged with black.

Years ago at Richardson a hungry fox came to feed at the Roadhouse. It came by night, over the snow, with its red fur and thick tail brush tipped with black and white hairs; and shyly, sometimes with a growl of mistrust, it gripped the meaty bone held out to it, and ran away into the darkness.

On Thanksgiving night a number of people from the neighborhood and from along the highway were gathered at the roadhouse to eat and drink, to sing and dance. The fox came that evening, got its ration, and was seen by all. Later, in a brief moment of quiet, a car was heard to stop on the road outside. Then, above the renewed noise of the music and talk, something like a muffled gunshot was heard, and the car drove on. Someone from the gathering went outdoors to investigate, and found a fresh pool of blood freezing in the roadside snow.

And again, on a Christmas night, we neighbors were gathered at the roadhouse. The snowfall that winter was deep against the outside wall, heaped under the eaves nearly to the level of the windowsill. It was a time of scarcity in the woods, when rabbits were few and the carnivores were hard-pressed to make a living.

During the course of the evening someone called out to the rest of the company, and we looked up from the bar to the window set high in the wall. A fullgrown coyote stood there in the houselight, looking down into the room. Gaunt and famished-looking in its grizzled, tawny fur, it stood for that moment framed in the window like a very accurate painting. The intense yellow eyes stared briefly into the light and the sudden quiet of the room. Then, realizing that it had been discovered, the grey ghost form turned and vanished.

An old friend and neighbor who lived on the far side of Birch Lake, some ten miles west of Richardson, for several years kept a pet woodchuck. It had been given to him when it was very young by a member of a survey crew who had found it strayed from its home burrow. Fed and nurtured, the animal grew fat and tame, tolerated by the one other member of the household, an aging husky.

Each fall, when the birch leaves had blown to the ground and the lake water began to freeze along the shoreline; when the first flurry of snow came drifting across the cold, dark lake, the woodchuck retreated to a den it had dug under a corner of the woodshed. Snow soon covered the entrance, and the woodchuck did not emerge until late in the following spring. It appeared then, blinking at the strong light, to sit in the sun and groom its thick, grizzled brown fur. And once more at home in the summer light, it moved about the yard in its chubby body, to search the patches of bare ground for fresh shoots and summer greens.

And early each summer, when its mating season arrived, the woodchuck took up a post on the chopping block or on top of the doghouse. Erect and watchful, it chattered and whistled, sending a piercing note over the meadow and into the nearby woods. But however long it sat and waited and whistled, no mate ever appeared. The woodchuck went into hibernation in a kind of tooth-muttering rage, to try again the following summer.

As it grew older, it became surly and aggressive, possessive of what it regarded as its home territory—the yard, the woodshed and the house—and strongly protective of its mixed human and canine family. With growing fierceness it attacked any stranger to the homestead, growling, clicking its big front teeth together in a loud and menacing way, and often chasing an unwary visitor into the house. To curb the creature, my friend sometimes found it necessary to corner it with a broom and drive it into the wire mink cage he kept handy. Once locked in, the woodchuck would rattle and rock and snarl and bite the wire, working itself into a greater rage, before it calmed down and went to sleep.

Finally, with regret, one day in late summer he herded the woodchuck into its cage. He took it by boat across the lake, and then by car to a wooded place several miles from home where he turned it loose. It never found its way back to Birch Lake. Its burly, chattering little presence was missed from time to time. We never knew if it survived alone in the country or, whether, foraging for itself on a dry and sunny slope, it finally found a mate and some late fulfillment of its baffled nature.

Early in my summer work at Richardson, while I was clearing trees on the hillside above the homestead yard, I heard a whimpering sound in the woods, a sound soulful and pathetic, like an abandoned baby crying. It seemed to come from a source close to the earth and not far from me, and yet I could not determine its location. I wondered if there was not a young bear close by whimpering for its mother, and I gazed apprehensively into the gloomy summer woods.

Sometime later, while visiting Fred Campbell, I described the sound and asked him what he thought it might be. He considered for a moment, then smiled and looked at me in that understanding, slightly superior way of his, and said that it was probably a porcupine looking for a mate. "They make that sound about this time of year, wandering in the woods. Seems like it can come from anywhere, and right out of the ground. I'll swear, you can look hard for the critter and not find it!"

Years later, on an early summer afternoon, I was walking back to the house from the mailbox when I again heard that plaintive, whimpering sound from somewhere on the dry hillside across the creek and somewhat below me. I decided then that I would attempt to call the animal to me and know for certain what it was.

I climbed down from the high shoulder of the road and crouched in a small cleared space at the edge of the alder brush. Putting my hands to my mouth, I began to call, imitating as well as I could that strange, intermittent crying. And very soon it seemed to me that the animal responded, that we were in communication.

When, in an interval of quiet, no cry came from the woods, I called and, once again, came a response. And soon I heard the sound of something scraping along through the brush, slowly and clumsily crushing last year's leaves under its feet. It stopped, then came on when I again imitated that plaintive crying.

And presently the grass and brush parted, and a large porcupine shoved its black nose into the open and stopped in front of me. It rose on its back legs and stood before me, no more than three feet away. It turned its head to one side so that one dark, unblinking eye regarded me suspiciously.

I kept absolutely still before that nearly blind, questioning gaze, and watched the blunt, black nose working in the air. The porcupine hesitated and leaned toward me as if it might come closer. I felt that with a little more encouragement it might have climbed into my lap, so close was it. But no. The mixed odors of the summer afternoon, combined and sorted by the black, twitching nostrils, found their way into the recesses of the small brain. The porcupine slowly dropped to the ground and turned to go. It hesitated, half-turned toward me, as if reluctant to give up the promise in the answering voice it had come to. But clearly something was not quite right about my khaki figure crouched there in the sunlight, something alien in the steady gaze that was fastened upon it. The porcupine pulled its yellowish, brindled weight into the woods once more. I heard the small crashing of leaves as it retreated, voiceless and betrayed.

On an October afternoon I was fishing in a channel of the Tanana River. The water was clear, with a small amount of drift ice running in the current. I stood on a sandbar not far from the wooded shoreline, working carefully with a pole and gaffhook; beside me on the snowy sandbar lay a number of red-skinned salmon.

As I stood there, paying close attention to the water and occasionally hooking a salmon, I thought I heard above the sound of the water and ice a scratching noise, and I felt that I was not alone. I turned around and looked up into the woods behind me. The sunlight was grey, diffused by clouds that late afternoon, but I could see in the shadows at the edge of the woods a large fallen poplar stretched out a few feet above the ground. And on top of the fallen tree a large lynx crouched. Its eyes were closed, and slowly and deliberately it was raking the claws of its forefeet in the dry bark of the tree. The animal seemed completely absorbed in what it was doing. I felt that were it not for the sound of the river at my back I could almost hear the big cat purring in a deep, throaty contentment.

The lynx paused in its raking. Its eyes opened, and it turned a wide yellow gaze upon me. There was no alarm in that look, no flash of recognition or fear. We looked at each other for a moment, each of us gazing into some dim shadow of ourselves. And then, not wanting to prolong my stare, as casually as I could I turned back to my fishing. When I looked again, the lynx was gone.

# Death Is a Meadowlark

LONG BEFORE I went to live in the woods my awareness of death seemed to have a depth beyond any exact recall. It existed as a memory composed of discontinuous images: a snake crushed on the summer roadway, reeking in the sun—how dull and flattened it was compared to the live snake, supple and glistening, I had seen in the grass a week before. A drowned and bloated frog I had pulled from the bottom of a backyard pool and held in my hand: a wonder—why did it not breathe? A bird in whose decaying nostrils small white worms were coiling. These were the naked things of an uninstructed childhood in which there was little instinctive fear.

And had I not seen as a child the crushed body of a woman sprawled at the city curbing? She had jumped from a window ledge many stories above, and lay concealed by the brown heap of her clothing. Nothing else was visible from where I stood, clutched by my mother on a crowded downtown street. There had been the sound of a scream, a sudden rush of air, a glimpse of a spread shape flying down, and the thudding shock of her landing. I was hurried away, and I saw no more.

And there had been also my own near death by drowning late in the first decade of my life. Death had taken the form of a watery green darkness into which I was sinking, slowed and numbed by the depth and cold, while above me the strange, lost sight of sunlight faded from the surface.

It was not then, but a later time, when I was about thirteen. We lived on the edge of uninhabited countryside at the end of a street in suburban California. From our backyard a pathway led uphill into open fields.

One Sunday morning in spring, after the family had returned from church and we had eaten a late breakfast, I went for a long walk alone over the fields. I do not remember what was on my mind then, confused by the unsorted emotions of youth or, as it may have been, delighting in the open sky and the sun on the warm grasses.

The pathway soon merged with a narrow country road. The bare soil in the wheeltracks was damp from the winter rains, and there was an occasional shallow pool of water in a deeper rut. As I came over the crest of the hill I saw something lying at the side of the road just ahead of me. When I came up to it, I saw that it was a rabbit, and that it was dead. Its brown and white fur was torn and its belly ripped open.

I came closer and stopped before it. Just for a moment I stood there looking down at the torn, but still intact animal. The blue bulge of its gut lay half-spilled from the body and shone brightly, glazed with blood, in the morning sunlight. A few flies already buzzed around it.

A nameless panic gripped me. I heard the buzzing of the flies and other insects, and somewhere close but out of sight a meadowlark was singing. There was nothing else around, no other sign of man, of animal or bird of prey. Beyond the hill crest not even a housetop showed above the yellow grasses. I was alone under the sun in an open field with death, unmistakable, physical death.

It was not just that still form lying at the edge of the road, nor the blood that was dried upon its fur; I had seen things like it before. It was something new—an awakening that fastened on the incredible shining blueness of the inside turned outside, the innermost part ripped from its place and spilled into the light where it did not belong. Gazing, fixed before it in the morning sunlight, I felt, perhaps for the first time, an absolute aloneness. And I who at that age loved solitude, knew that this was death, the loneliest solitude of all.

In terror I began to walk, away from that scene, over the grassy slope of the hill, but looking behind me all the while as if I expected that quiet, mutilated form to rise from the damp ground and follow me. Perhaps I feared that somewhere in that silent, sunny countryside, in the grass, even in the voice of the meadowlark, death itself was waiting.

I do not know what sermon I had half-listened to that morning in church; something that had deepened my mood and prompted my walk—something about mortality, was it, of death and the hereafter, of reward and damnation? I don't remember. Yet somehow I felt deeply that I was guilty, but of what I did not know.

I walked a long way that morning, troubled and confused. I returned over the same path on my way home. As fearful as I had been, both repelled and attracted, I had to see that form of death again. I had to know.

But when I came again to that place in the road, on the rounded hilltop, there was nothing there. I looked around, thinking I had mistaken the location, and that the dead rabbit was somewhere close by. Its absence now was even more alarming. Had I really seen it? But yes, for here in the brown soil at the edge of the grass was a small, darkened spot that appeared to be blood, and near it a little patch of rabbit fur.

I struggled with explanations. Something—hawk or fox—disturbed originally by my coming, had run off and left its victim in the road. And when I had gone, it returned to claim its food.

Still the feeling of dread remained as I walked on toward home. I think now that I told no one of what I had seen, but kept it as a secret, something shared between me, the grass, and the unseen meadowlark. The impression of that morning stayed with me for a long time, and for a while I avoided that part of the road on my walks. When later I crossed the hill at that spot, alone or with friends, I half-expected to see the rabbit again, to have it rise before me from the grass without warning, and with that large, incredibly distended bulge of its stomache, veined with fat, gleaming so brightly blue and green in the sun. But a ghost-image was all I had; a latent emotion charged with mistrust, and a lingering fear.

Transitory in the field, under the sun, slowly disintegrating under blows of the summer rain, an image of the world's stupendous accident. An instant of inexplicable calm, as on the bright, cold winter day I found a redpoll frozen on a snowbank at the entrance to the homestead road. There was nothing to tell me how the bird came to die there. It may have been stunned by the wind gust from a passing car, or it may have fallen asleep while feeding on the blown seeds of the few weed stalks that showed above the snow, and momentarily warming itself in the cold sun. There was not a mark on its body, not a feather disturbed. Under the downy fluff the tiny feet were stiffened; the eyes were half-closed and crystalized; at either side of the nostrils lay a delicate whisker of frost. The rusty crown of its head was bright with color, and the flushed breast seemed almost warm to my touch. But it was absolutely still, the breast and the heart within it joined in a lump of ice. I held the bird for a moment before putting it to rest again in the snow. It seemed to weigh nothing at all.

In that tiny, quenched image of vitality, a bird like a leaf dropped by the wind in passing, I felt something of our common, friable substance—a shared vulnerability grasped once with insight and passion, and then too easily forgotten. Necessarily forgotten, perhaps, for to keep such a thing constantly before one might be intolerable; the identification would wound too deeply.

I see again the worn, chalk-white skull of a caribou left behind on the fall tundra many years ago. One half of an antler poked up from the deep moss in which the skull was lying; the moss and the accumulation of old leaves and plant debris had nearly buried the rest of it from view.

When I tilted the skull slightly, I saw that a thin, green mold clung to the bone below the soil line. There had been no trace there for a long time of meat, of marrow or gristle. All else was bleached, chalky and crumbling: the upper jaw with a few loose molars, the long thin nostril bone, the eye-sockets, and the mouldering hollows behind the ears. The remaining antler revealed the worn tooth-marks of rodents who in past years, when the skull was still fresh, had gnawed it for the calcium in the bone.

The small lichens and the mosses that had taken root upon the skull were breaking down whatever was left of its structure. It seemed to me as I walked away and turned to view it from a little distance, that the skull was like a small vessel, abandoned by captain and crew; rudderless and demasted, it was sinking into the moss and frozen sod. The wet, green sea-life of the tundra washed over the pale wreck in tiny waves year after year, and sooner or later sun, rain and frost would claim it completely. Farewell.

On a snowy day early in October I was sitting at breakfast alone in the house at Richardson, gloomy with the knowledge that the moose season had closed and I had yet to get my meat for the winter. I had hunted for better than two weeks, all through the cool, dry days of late September, and had seen nothing but tracks. Winter was coming, there was snow on the ground, nearly eight inches of it already, and I knew that in order to find a moose now I would have to go far into the hills for it, and by the time I got it, late in the rut, the meat was sure to be lean and tough.

As I was cleaning up the breakfast pans and dishes, I thought I heard a sound outside, rather like a low grunt, and one of the dogs chained in the yard gave a sharp "woof." I went to the door and looked out. To my astonishment I saw a large bull moose stalking slowly uphill through the snowy garden.

The moose, plainly in view against the white, cleared ground, paused and looked down toward the house and yard. In those few moments of what seemed to be a kind of mutual recognition, it struck me that the moose was not in the best of condition, that perhaps it had been beaten in a fight, or was overtaken by weariness. But no matter—here was my meat, and right in the yard.

I had a rifle at my hand, but at that moment a car went by on the road below the house, driving slowly because of the fresh snowfall. As keenly as I wanted that moose, I feared that it would be seen if I shot it there in plain view and out of season. I waited, and watched the moose climb the open hill and go out of sight over the crest toward the potato patch.

I decided immediately to follow it, to take another way up the hill and head it off, since the moose seemed to be in no hurry. I dressed myself quickly in overshoes, cap, jacket and gloves, and with the rifle in hand I took off up the hill through the falling snow.

I climbed through the woods, following a trail I had cut the year before. I did not dare to stop for rest, but plowed on, hoping that the snowfall and the laden branches would dampen any sound I was making. In a short time I reached the top of a narrow ridge where the trail began to level off. And there I found the tracks of the moose who had just passed before me. He could not be far ahead. Panting, stumbling at times in the fresh snow, I followed those tracks, determined to catch up with that moose or fall in the snow from trying.

Within a quarter of a mile I came to a place where the trail straightened and I could see some distance ahead of me. Another twenty yards, and I caught up with the moose, now a large brown bulk blurred by the falling snow, standing in the birches. He was stopped in the

55

trail, his head half-turned, looking back in my direction.

Trembling from the long climb, I raised the rifle, trying for some kind of shooting rest against the nearest tree. As I was doing this, the moose, alerted now, broke into a trot and began to move swiftly ahead. I had no time for a better shot; he would soon be out of sight, and I was too badly winded from the climb to pursue him any further. I aimed for a spot just below the tail stump and fired.

At the sound of the shot the moose jumped, ran forward at a faster pace, and stopped. As I approached him, he turned to one side of the trail and stepped slowly into the woods, as if he would think awhile on what had happened. In the one large, dark eye turned toward me I could see a kind of blunted panic and bewilderment. I was ready to shoot again, not knowing if I really had him, when he staggered, felt for better footing, and fell heavily on his right side with a soft, cushioned *swoosh,* sending a shower of dry snow into the air. Once he tried to raise his head then let it fall. As I came near I saw his chest heave out a mighty sigh, and one leg stiffen slightly. And then the woods were silent in the falling snow.

The open eye of the moose gazed blank and dull into the tree-stroked whiteness. A few wet flakes fell on the eyelids, melted on the warm nostrils, and sank into the long, unmoving ears.

The great, dark bulk was still. I felt, as I always do at such times, a strange and painful combination of emotions, if what one feels then can be called emotion precisely—a mingling of awe, of regret, of elation and relief. There was a quiet space in which to breathe, to acknowledge that something urgent and needed had been accomplished, all anxiety and uncertainty for the moment done with.

I returned down the snowy trail to the house to get my knife, my axe and saw, and a length of rope. And once more up the trail, I was soon at work on the carcass. First, I cut off the head with its heavy antlers. Then I tied a foreleg to a tree, and pushed and balanced the heavy, inert bulk onto its back. As always, it was strenuous work for a single man. But now death was forgotten. A transformation had taken place, and what had been a vital and breathing creature, capable of perception and of movement, was now only meat and salvage—a hairy mound of bone and muscle.

When I cut through the hide and strained inner tissue of the paunch, a cloud of red steam burst on the snowy air. And soon I could see deep into the steaming red cavity divided from the upper torso by the taut, muscular wall of the diaphragm. Working by feel alone in the hot soupiness of the rib cage, I loosened the windpipe, then pulled the stomache and the intestines clear, tumbling the heavy, stretched bag and ropy folds onto the snow. There was no fat on the veil nor around the kidneys, but I had not expected to find any. The meat would be lean, but it was better than no meat at all.

And now, with the entire inner part open to the light, I found that my single bullet had traveled the length of the body cavity, just under the spine, and had cut the blood vessels around the heart. Death had been swift, and little meat was spoiled.

That afternoon I dragged the quarters downhill through the snow and hung them on the rack behind the house. A week later a strong wind blew from the south, much of the snow melted, and a springlike warmth sailed through the woods. Where the killed moose had lain, the shaded snow thawed, then froze again, forming a kind of sunken circle that was stained pink and yellow, and matted with hair and leaves. It was soon to be covered by a fresh snowfall, and in a far month to come, to melt and be once more a part of the spring earth.

# Ice

FOR SOME TIME now in the woods, away from the sun, in ravines and hollows where the ground is normally wet, the soil has darkened and is hard and cold to the touch. The deep, shaded mosses have stiffened, and there are tiny crystals of ice in their hairy spaces.

Water has sunken in the pools of the footpaths; in the high ridge trails the small potholes are ringed with transparent ice, or they filled with whitened splinters shattered by the foot of some passing animal. Ice thickened with leaves surrounds a circle of open water in the flowing pool of the creek below the house.

The waters are freezing. From the reedy shallows outward to the centers of the roadside ponds: black ice, clear and hard, with bubbles that are white; opaque patches of shell ice that shatter easily when stepped on. The last ducks that kept to the open centers of the ponds are gone. Clumps of stiff dry grass stand upright there, held fast, casting their shadows on the evening ice.

Now that the steady frost has come, I have been thinking about the river. It is time to take a walk over the sandbars and islands, while there is still so little snow. It is late October, and the smaller channels of this broad and braided river have long since stopped flowing, and their remaining pools are frozen. Far out in mid-river, beyond the big, wooded island, a single large channel is now the only open water. The sound of that water, though distant, comes strong and pervasive over the dry land dusted with snow: a deep and swallowed sound, as if the river had ice in its throat.

One afternoon I take the steep path downhill to the riverbed. I make my way across to the big island over sandbar and dusty ice, past bleached piles of driftwood and through waist-high willows and alders, to the gravelly, ice-coated shore of the open channel. I walk a short distance out on the shore ice and stand there, looking at the water. A little wind comes down the wide river, over the frozen bars, smelling of winter.

Free of its summer load of silt, the water is clear in the shallows, incredibly blue and deep in the middle of the channel. Ice is riding in the water, big rafts of it crowding each other, falling through the rapids above me and catching on the bottom stones. Here where the current slackens and deepens, the water is heavy and slow with ice, with more and more ice.

Call it mush ice, or pan ice. It forms at night and during the colder days in the slack water of eddies and shallows: a cold slush that gathers weight and form. Drifting and turning in the backwaters, it is pulled piecemeal into the main current and taken down.

Now on the heavy water great pans of ice are coming, breaking and reforming, drifting with the slowed current: shaggy donuts of ice, ragged squares and oblongs, turning and pushing against each other, islands of ice among lakes of dark blue water. Crowded shoreward by the current, they brush the shore ice with a steady "shsss" as they catch and go by. And with each sheering contact a little of that freezing slush clings to the outer edge of the shore ice. The ice is building outward, ridged and whitened, thickening with each night of frost, with each wave of shallow water that washes it.

---

As I look intently into the shallows, I see that boulder ice, a soft, shapeless and gluey mass, is forming on some large, rounded stones not far below the surface; the river is freezing from the bottom also. Now and then a piece of that water-soaked ice dislodges and comes to the surface, turning over and over. It is dirty ice, grey and heavy with sand, small stones and debris.

Where it gathers speed in the rapids above, the sound of all this ice and water is loud, rough, and vaguely menacing. As the cold gradually deepens and the sunlight departs in the days to come, the floating ice will become harder and thicker, and the sound of its movement in the water will change to a harsher grinding and crushing. Now in the slowed current before me, it is mostly that steady and seething "shsss" that I hear, and underneath it a softer clinking as of many small glasses breaking against each other.

Standing here, watching the ice come down, I recall past years when I came to a channel much like this one, in mid-October with only an inch or two of snow on the gravel bars, to fish for salmon. I had with me a long pole with a steel hook at one end. Standing very still and quiet where the current slackened against the ice, I watched for the glowing red and pink forms of salmon on their way upriver in the last run of the season. Sometimes I caught sight of one toward mid-channel, beyond reach of my pole; but often they traveled slowly along the edge of the ice, finning and resting, at times nearly motionless in the current. And carefully I extended my gaffhook along the ice edge behind the fish, and with a sudden, strong sweep and jerk I struck the fish through its body and flung it ashore.

The big hook made a nasty gash in the side of the salmon, and fish blood soon stained the snow where I piled them, one by one. If the fish was a female heavy with eggs, the eggs sometimes spilled through the torn side of the fish, to lie pink and golden in the shallow snow with the glazed, mottled bodies of the freezing salmon.

There was something grand and barbaric in that essential, repeated act. To stand there in the snow and cold air toward the end of the year, with a long hook poised above the ice-filled river, was to feel oneself part of something so old that its origin was lost in the sundown of many winters: a feeling intensified, made rich by the smell of ice and cold fish-slime, by the steely color of the winter sky, and the white snow stained with the redness of the salmon: the color of death and the color of winter. And to all this was added the strong black of the ravens that gathered each evening as I was leaving the river, to clean the snow of the spilled eggs and blood.

I caught the big fish one at a time, watching and walking quietly along the edge of the ice, hour after hour. In a few days I had from two to three hundred salmon heaped in scattered mounds in the thin, dry snow of the sandbar, to be packed home a few at a time, heavy and frozen.

I see no salmon now as I stand here by this ice-filled channel, searching its green, bouldery shadows and bluer depths for a telltale flash of crimson. It may be that there is not a good run this fall, that I am too early or too late, or that the fish have taken another way upriver.

---

The sound of the water and the ice before me is one sound, familiar over the years. But there are other sounds of the ice, among them the strange and eerie moaning that comes from under the new ice of the pond when it is walked on, as if some sad spirit in the depth of the pond were trying to speak. In midwinter, a large sheet of ice will split with a rippling crack when the temperature suddenly changes or the ice bed shifts underneath, the ripple traveling fast with a winnowing sound at the end. And there are those small ticking sounds of the ice in the evening when the cold slides toward its deepest zero, as if a thousand hidden insects were chirping bitterly in chorus under the ice and snow. And, finally, the thundering crack and plunge of the shelf ice breaking off in the spring as the rising water wears away its support, a sound that can be heard for miles, like the detonation of a heavy building.

The ice sings, groans, howls and whistles like a living thing. Years ago while hunting caribou in the Alaska Range, I heard the oldest lament of the ice. It was early in October, and the slow freeze was coming down over the empty land and its many lakes. As I stood alone and listening by the roadside one afternoon, I heard on the nearly windless air, as if from the earth itself, a muted and forsaken moaning from the lakes and ponds. It was a sound out of prehistory, of something deeply wounded and abandoned, slowly giving up its life to the cold. There were fleeting ghost-fires on the tundra, white-maned shadows from the bands of caribou fleeing before something I could not see. Then, distant shots, gunfire, the sound of a truck rattling by on the frozen road.

Here before me the river is still awake, still speaking in its half-choked mutter and murmur, still surging, pushing its ice-filled way across the open sand and gravel. But one day—it may be soon, or it may be very late, when the solstice sun clears the south horizon—the sound of all this surging and grinding, this shredding and crushing will stop. The great silence will have come, that other sound of the ice, which is almost nothing at all. This channel will have finally filled, the last open water will close, and the river will go under the ice. Snow will drift and cover the ice I stand on.

If I were to walk out here in midwinter, the only sound I would be likely to hear would be the wind, pushing snow across the ice. Only now and then, while walking over the frozen shallows, would I hear under my feet the sound of trickling water finding its way somehow through the ice. And later still, when ice has thickened to a depth of many feet on the deepest channel, I might hear far down in some snow-filled crevice the deep murmur and surge of the river running beneath me.

For the ice and the river under it are never still for long. Again and again throughout this long winter, water will find its way into the open, welling up from a seam in the ice, and spreading over the existing surface of ice and snow to freeze again in a perilous sheet. The wind will bring its dry snow to polish the new ice and turn it into a great slick and glare. Delicate flowers of frost will bloom upon it: small, glittering blossoms standing curled and fragile on the gritty ice, to be scattered by the first passage of air. And over the renewed expanse of ice there will be silence again, the silence of ice, unchanged since the first winter of Earth.

---

But all this is still to come, as it has come before. Winter is making its way across the land, over slope and plain, bog and high meadow, across lake and pond, outlet and feeder. It has progressed slowly this fall in an even, majestic tread, with a little more frost each night, a little less warmth each day. Meanwhile, the open water of the river flows at my feet, steady and heavy with ice, the deep sound of it filling the landscape around me.

I turn and walk back to the home shore whose tall yellow bluffs still bare of snow I can see nearly half a mile to the north. I find my way as I came, over dusty sandbars and by old channels, through shrubby stands of willows. The cold, late afternoon sun breaks through its cloud cover and streaks the grey sand mixed with snow.

As it has fallen steadily in the past weeks, the river has left behind many shallow pools, and these are now roofed with ice. When I am close to the main shore I come upon one of them, not far from the wooded bank. The light snow that fell a few days ago has blown away; the ice is polished and is thick enough to stand on. I can see to the bottom without difficulty, as through heavy, dark glass.

I bend over, looking at the debris caught there in the clear, black depth of the ice: I see a few small sticks, and many leaves. There are alder leaves, roughly-toothed and still half green; the more delicate birch leaves and aspen leaves, the big, smooth poplar leaves, and narrow leaves from the willows. They are massed or scattered, as they fell quietly or as the wind blew them into the freezing water. Some of them are still fresh in color, glowing yellow and orange; others are mottled with grey and brown. A few older leaves lie sunken and black on the silty bottom. Here and there a pebble of quartz is gleaming. But nothing moves there. It is a still, cold world, something like night, with its own fixed planets and stars.